IMAGES
of Aviation

BUNKER HILL AND
GRISSOM AIR FORCE BASE

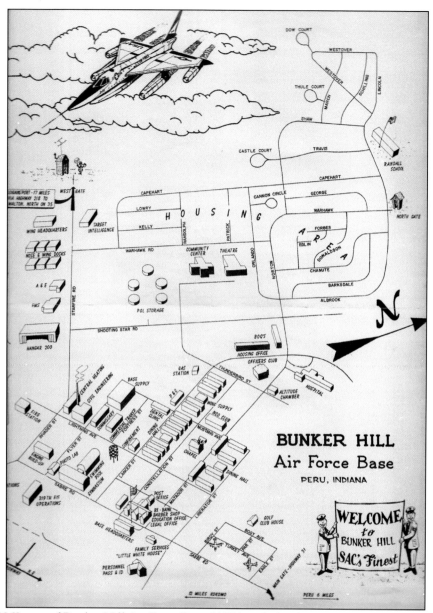

This 1962 map of Bunker Hill Air Force Base (AFB) includes the new "Arnold Acres" housing project, where most of the streets are named after deceased Air Force heroes. Indiana governor Matthew Welsh wrote to base personnel in 1962: "It is comforting to know that America, although dedicated to peace, is nevertheless fully prepared to retaliate swiftly and with finality in the event of armed attack." (Courtesy of the Grissom Air Museum.)

ON THE COVER: A bizarre runway accident during an alert drill at Bunker Hill AFB killed Manuel "Rocky" Cervantes, third from right, and resulted in a "Broken Arrow" nuclear weapons incident in December 1964. The radioactive wreckage of Rocky's bomber remained buried on the base for 36 years. From left to right are William James, Robert Causey, Dale Younger, Rocky, Roger Hall, and Fred Wood. Hall and pilot Leary Johnson, not pictured, escaped the accident with minor burns. (Courtesy of Shamaine Pleczko.)

IMAGES
of Aviation

BUNKER HILL AND GRISSOM AIR FORCE BASE

Tom Kelley
Introduction by Col. Alan Dugard, USAF (Ret.)

ARCADIA
PUBLISHING

Published by Arcadia Publishing
Charleston, South Carolina

Printed in the United States of America

Library of Congress Control Number: 2015943781

For all general information, please contact Arcadia Publishing:
Telephone 843-853-2070
Fax 843-853-0044
E-mail sales@arcadiapublishing.com
For customer service and orders:
Toll-Free 1-888-313-2665

Visit us on the Internet at www.arcadiapublishing.com

"In the long history
of the world, only a
few generations have
been granted the role
of defending freedom
in its maximum
hour of danger."
—Pres. John F. Kennedy,
January 20, 1961.

CONTENTS

FOREWORD

I have had a lengthy association with Grissom Air Base beginning in 1973, and I am pleased to contribute some of my photographs and introductory words to Tom Kelley's pictorial history of Grissom. The Cold War encompassed much of Grissom's history to include fighters, bombers, and tankers and thousands of airmen and their families assigned there. On the surface, air bases are just concrete, buildings, and equipment, but they are best remembered because of the people who lived and worked there. They shared important missions, shouldered the load, and succeeded on behalf of all of us. They laughed, cried, complained, worried, sweated, and froze together. And so, Grissom is much more than just an air base—it is a special place and time for so many, a reminder of the mighty Strategic Air Command (SAC), the "Red" commies, a culture filled with Air Force language, ORIs (Operational Readiness Inspections), wailing klaxon alerts, the smell of jet fuel, around-the-clock jet noise, lookalike base housing, Officer and NCO Club parties, gate guards, deployments, homecomings, and so much more. No matter what squadron, active or reserve, or whether one was working in operations, maintenance, or support, the camaraderie was unique and lasting, and the names Bunker Hill or Grissom immediately bring back memories and create images in our minds almost like old black-and-white movies. For so long, there was nothing beautiful about Grissom, it was primarily a hodge-podge of old World War II– and Cold War–era buildings, and one can still see evidence of that. Fortunately, the portion serving today as Grissom Air Reserve Base, currently Indiana's only official air base, is a fully revamped, state-of-the-art tanker base. Regardless, I can still drive by my old, now vacant, squadron building and remember all the good times, the friends, and the excitement. Unfortunately, many don't have that opportunity or their memories are fading, and so it is a blessing that Tom Kelley authored this gem of a book to help take us back to that special place in time. Grissom holds a place in my heart, and I hope you enjoy reading this book as much as I do.

—Col. Tim Cahoon, USAF (Ret.)

An A-10 and KC-135 pilot, Colonel Cahoon, call sign "Kaboom," flew with the 434th Tactical Fighter Wing (TAC) and later commanded the 305th Air Refueling Wing (SAC).

ACKNOWLEDGMENTS

To anyone who shares my affection for the people, the mission, and the aircraft of the Strategic Air Command in general, and Grissom Air Force Base in particular, a collection of base photographs is pretty exciting. I would like to express my thanks to everybody who served in SAC during the entire history of the command.

The B-58 Hustler Association, the Air Force Association, social media, and the Grissom Air Museum deserve special thanks for connecting me with the veteran airmen, Air Force families, and real historians who provided perspective and material for this book. A thank-you is owed to Debbie Anspach, Ray Bensch, Bill Bergdoll, Howard Bialas, Hank Bolger, Arley Brewer, B.J. Brown, Tim Cahoon, Curt Christensen, Paul Coffey, Wayne Coker, Alan Dugard, John Ensign, Jim Frankenfield, Andy Garrison, Jeff Gilland, Duane Gordon, Joseph Guastella, "Dutch" Holland, George Holt, Max Jordan, Al Kanauka, John Kelley, Mike Kelley, Jon Kitchel, Sid and Joey Kubesch, Sharon Kehler Michaels, Robert Luesse, Jon Mickley, Richard Mulcher, Aungelic Nelson, Shemaine Pleczko, Jim Price, Kathleen Reade, Annie Robb, John Roth, Elgin Shaw, Brenda Shepherd, Elmer Slavey, Jack Strank, Tom Thompson, Anthony Trzeciak, Craig Trott, Troy Warner, and Terry Wyant. I hope that I've done justice to your contributions.

It's probably also a good idea to acknowledge the patience of my beautiful and long-suffering wife, Teresa. She was always willing to let me off with little more than a condescending smile while I visited the Grissom Air Museum, drank coffee with Jack Strank, or beer with Tim Cahoon under the pretense of "working."

Claiming no current affiliation with the US Air Force, every picture in this book, unless noted otherwise, are official declassified US Air Force photographs from the Grissom Air Museum collection. Any opinions, unless credited to a specific source, are my own and may or may not be taken seriously, just like they were while I was in the Air Force. Since an airman's rank changed every so often, I avoided mentioning it except in the case of historically recognized individuals. If anybody's offended, I'm sorry.

I hope you enjoy this photographic tribute to the Bunker Hill and Grissom airmen, their aircraft, their mission, and their ultimate victory in preserving peace through deterrence.

INTRODUCTION

This is the story of a place, a base, flight crews, and one great plane—Bunker Hill/Grissom Air Force Base.

Having completed my B-58 lead-in training in the similarly delta wing F-102 at Perrin Air Force Base in Texas, I went back to New Hampshire to pick up my family and begin the most enjoyable flying experience of my Air Force career. As a family, we were excited about going to Bunker Hill AFB in Peru, pronounced PEEru.

It was late March and very cold, and a thin layer of snow was on the ground. As we approached the entrance to the base, the turn-in was not noticeable, and I inadvertently passed by it. I would have to go to the next intersection to make a U-turn. As we got to that point, I was stunned to see elephants roaming behind fences in the field diagonally across the road. Elephants? This was my first impression of the neighboring community of this historic base, once owned and run by the Navy, and later to be named after Gus Grissom, who was killed during training as an astronaut. As it turned out, Peru was the winter home of the Ringling Bros. and Barnum & Bailey circus, thus elephants had a place in the history of this base.

My crew very quickly became totally immersed in the training needed to be a qualified combat crew in the B-58. The Combat Crew Training Squadron (CCTS) would own the three new crews and extra pilot who had recently arrived and were going to make sure we were capable of flying the most complicated and fastest bomber ever made. Despite the fact that I had over 3,000 hours total flying time, we were the FNGs. Our experience was good for a cup of coffee and nothing else.

To become one of those elite Hustler crewmembers, you had to undergo severe scrutiny and a thorough selection process. You were recommended by your wing commander, and then, the SAC hierarchy would make the final decision. Once chosen, you were given crew members, a navigator-bombardier, and a Defensive Systems Operator (DSO). We would fly a series of "flights" in simulators before even getting close to a real airplane. The simulator rides were programmed to go over the basics of the aircraft, such as takeoff and landing and managing the 14,000 gallons of jet fuel to maintain a flyable center of gravity at supersonic speeds. Student pilots used the simulator to experience every phase of B-58 flying, peppered with emergencies in every system of the aircraft. Each student crew was assigned a CCTS instructor crew; my instructor pilot (IP) was Buck Carroll, a slow-talking individual who, as I discovered, was a super pilot and a tireless instructor serious about his role. After five "sim" rides, the pilot and DSO would take their first ride in a TB-58, a Hustler that had been modified to accommodate an instructor pilot.

Having flown other aircraft that you took off by merely pulling back on the control column, the first rotation of the B-58 using a stick, with the nose coming up 12 degrees, was a shock. This aircraft could fly! Pushing the four J-79 engines into afterburner and accelerating to 425 knots while climbing 3,000 or 4,000 feet per minute had the same effect as being tied to a rocket. Accelerating to 1.67 Mach to climb for a supersonic run was experiencing a new world of flight. Air refueling in the B-58 was much different than what I had experienced in the B-47. The wide delta wing made for a very stable platform, and the engine power seemed limitless. Using only one inboard engine, I could hold position with the tanker even when completely weighed down with fuel.

Mistakes in the simulator rides were necessary learning experiences that paid off in the TB rides and, later, B rides. Rotating too early led to instant disaster. Landings were at high speed, usually above 160 knots, as there were no flaps on the B-58, and they had their own flair procedures. For example, as soon as you touched down, you deployed a drag chute and lifted the nose to apply aerodynamic braking. B rides with an instructor pilot in the bombardier-navigator station came after four TB rides. This was a critical period in our training and would end with a celebration after the crew landed their first solo ride. A series of full-crew rides would follow, and the training would end with the crew being declared "combat ready."

Being combat ready meant you could pull the seven day nuclear alert, a fact all the other crews cheered, as time in the "hole" came about all too often. The more combat-ready crews, the less alert! For most crews, this meant one week out of three you would reside across the runway in the underground windowless structure known as the Alert Facility. It was guarded and surrounded by barbed-wire fences, and you were unable to do anything without your crew. Access to other parts of the base, such as the theater and gym, was possible, but the housing area was off limits. Your aircraft was loaded with nuclear bombs and each aircraft was housed in a "Hustler hut," which kept them out of the elements but plugged in and capable of launching an entire force of B-58s in a matter of minutes.

Training for this possibility came in the form of practice alerts. They were called Alpha, Bravo, and Coco alerts. Klaxons were a way of life for anyone who ever spent time in a "mole hole." They would cause rapid movement by all crews to their vehicles, and the race was on. Alert drills were only conducted by order of SAC to test the wing's readiness and could come at any time of the day or night. There was always the chance this would be a real war, known as a Red Dot. Locked in every alert aircraft was an encrypted message designating our targets. If we were not ordered to stand down from an alert drill, we unlocked these messages, verified them with the other crew members, and flew to our Positive Control Turn-around Point (PCTAP). Unlike the movies, we could not proceed beyond our PCTAP, or "failsafe" point, and go on to our targets unless we received a specific "go code" from SAC.

On the other side of the coin, we always hoped it would be an ordinary Alpha alert, called a Blue Dot message, meaning that we only had to start engines and go through a shutdown, and then go back to the hole. All alert drills were timed for crew reaction, and it was imperative that we met timing criteria. A Coco alert was the most stressful, as it meant you had to start engines and proceed through a simulated launch, taking the runway, bringing power up, and then taxiing to the end of the runway, taxiing back, and returning to the Hustler hut. This exercise could take hours for all aircraft to be repositioned; therefore, every crew tried to be the first out of their hut so they could be the first to be repositioned. Tail-end Charlie would have that long wait. The saying was "light the fires and first one out was lead."

Alert became a bonding exercise for all, not just within your own crew, but also among other crews, and funny things would and could happen. It did not take much for an individual or a crew to become the object of attention, as it seemed easy to have what you may have done with a simple misdeed on an alert exercise become a weeklong briefing item. One such incident happened on a Coco alert night, when one pilot, in his haste to be first coming out of his Hustler hut, brought his throttles up through the stop for full power and lit his afterburner in one engine. Needless to say, it lit up the entire alert area, scattered a number of crew chiefs and power carts, and scared the entire taxiing force. There was no real harm done, but the pilot will never be forgotten, and the remainder of his week on alert was not comfortable. The nickname "Torch" will ever be applicable. There was no end to the interplay among crews. It was the competitive nature of a bunch of professionals that led us to be what we were, and we were damn good!

The base gym was very close to the runway and the Alert Facility and was always open to alert crews. Aircrews took advantage of the indoor running track and the two excellent handball courts, especially in the cold winters. It also was a very good place to meet your family, as they could get away from the house and see their husband and dad. It was a relief for the wives, as they had to fend for themselves when we were on alert. The families could even use the spacious pool; crews could not.

As I gained experience in the aircraft, I became an instructor pilot and, later, was placed into the CCTS where I would train the new pilots coming into the aircraft. It was there that the beauty of the airplane really took hold. Training a new pilot in the B-58 was an exercise in precise flying from the backseat.

To slow down during a landing, a B-58 lands with her nose in the air, using the delta wings to reduce airspeed and lift. It's a great aerodynamic concept, except that you can't see the runway around the nose. To further complicate the important operation of landing the TB-58, the instructor pilot, who was positioned behind the student in tandem, had to unstrap from his seat and pull himself up to look over the pilot's ejection capsule. The closer you got to the ground, the less you could see, so you had to look to both sides to make sure you had the aircraft in the middle of the runway and not on one of the edges.

Takeoffs and landings in the nose-high attitude were somewhat challenging for pilots who were used to flying the B-52, which was so big it always seemed to be parallel with the ground. But compared to the B-52, aerial refuelings in the Hustler were pretty comfortable. Supersonic flight was given to the student usually on their second TB ride, and part of that was an instructor demonstration of an engine failure of an outboard engine at Mach 2. I always held my breath during that demonstration. The sudden yank of an outboard throttle from the afterburner "overspeed" position to idle always was done holding my breath. Obviously, it always worked!

Bunker Hill/Grissom AFB was a place of beginnings and endings. The memories linger, and the friends remain. Most are seen at reunions for those who flew in the magnificent Hustler. It was a special airplane, flown from a special base. I was so fortunate to have been a part of the experience.

—Col. Alan Dugard, USAF (Ret.)

Colonel Dugard is also a B-52 combat pilot who commanded the 307th Strategic Wing, U-Tapao Air Base Thailand during the closing days of the Vietnam War. He is the author of When the Wolf Rises, *a personal account of the Linebacker bombing missions over North Vietnam.*

One

Bunker Hill Bluejackets

During World War II, which involved the United States from 1941 until 1945, the aircraft carrier and naval airpower assumed at least equal importance with the battleship in fleet operation. From a 1939 system of 11 inadequate air stations and eight reserve bases, the Navy grew its Air Force to 27,500 airplanes during the war. Pilots were needed as fast as American industry could build the airplanes, and more than $10 million was spent for construction at each of 38 new air stations. Bunker Hill was one of them.

The first enlisted man to arrive, John Howell, received his orders for transfer to Peru, Indiana, on April Fool's Day 1942. Traveling with Chief Aviation Machinist Joe Bealor, they checked in at the Indiana Bar in downtown Peru before looking for the base. "We knew it was the place because there were two tool shacks, five outhouses and what looked like 100 WPA boys leaning on their shovels."

A young and harried lieutenant was running things from the telephone office in Peru; so for the first few weeks, it would be up to the two chiefs to organize the construction crews and newly arriving sailors. Recruits reported to a farmhouse along US 31 and, before even receiving uniforms, were put to work building four 5,000-foot concrete runways and a 2,500-foot landing mat. Barracks and messing facilities were constructed to accommodate 800 students and 1,800 permanent personnel, a number that eventually swelled to 6,300. Thousands of Navy, Marine Corps, and Coast Guard pilots learned to fly at Bunker Hill. More than 3,000 US Navy airmen were killed in combat.

Having helped win the war, Bunker Hill Naval Air Station was deactivated in 1946. The sailors went home, airplanes were sold at salvage prices, tools and furniture evaporated, and control of the installation was turned over to a local committee for economic development.

While grass grew up from cracks in the landing mat, and the pool was used to store a bountiful soybean harvest, most of the base was swallowed up in Miami County agriculture.

Just a month after the Navy broke ground for Bunker Hill Naval Air Station on April 28, 1942, 35 percent of the buildings were completed, and 10 percent of the concrete runway was down. The base was officially commissioned on July 1, 1942, when the first American flag was hoisted above the installation.

Robert Miles of Winchester, Indiana, reported to Bunker Hill in July 1942 and traveled back and forth by bus from Kokomo every day. "I remember the mud at Bunker Hill. It must have been the only place in the world where you could stand in the mud and get dust in your eyes."

Acquisition of the 2,000 acres that would become, at least initially, the US Naval Reserve Aviation Base, Peru, Indiana, was completed in April 1942. Recruits were quartered in Peru and Kokomo and mustered every morning at a brick farmhouse along US 31. The base was rechristened as Bunker Hill Naval Air Station (NAS) in March 1943. The great pool pictured here was finished in October.

Since the US Navy does most of its business on the water, and Indiana is hundreds of miles from the nearest ocean, Bunker Hill NAS hosted what, at that time, was the second-largest indoor swimming pool in the world. Hundreds of skinny, pale, and hopeful naval aviators were trained and tested year-round at the "USS *Cornfield*."

Women Accepted for Voluntary Emergency Service (WAVES) was established on July 30, 1942, as a World War II division of the US Naval Reserve. Consisting entirely of women, "emergency" implied that the acceptance of females was due to the unusual circumstances of World War II, and at the end of the war, they would not be allowed to continue in naval service. The first WAVES, all ensigns, arrived at Bunker Hill NAS on June 22, 1943. By 2012, 52,000 women were serving on active duty in the Navy.

Comdr. Morton Seligman was awarded his second Navy Cross for valor when the USS *Lexington* was sunk by the Japanese navy during the Battle of the Coral Sea. Two months later, he was given command of Bunker Hill NAS while the Navy investigated him for releasing top-secret information to a newspaper reporter. He avoided a court martial by retiring from the Navy before the war's end. Seligman is pictured at the base with Peru mayor J.O. Miller (right) in 1943.

Capt. D.D. Gurley reported aboard as the new commanding officer in July 1943. Gurley had landed the first Navy airplane and commanded another inland naval air station near Ottumwa, Iowa, before being promoted and reassigned to Indiana. Kokomo mayor Charles Orr presented the captain with the key to the city at a Navy Day luncheon in October.

The base gymnasium was built next door to the pool with the goal of providing an indoor exercise and training area for aviation cadets and other naval personnel. Large rolling doors on one side of the huge Quonset building proved useful when additional storage space was needed for the war effort. On the basketball court is a Vultee SNV trainer, similar in proportions but slower than the Navy's version of the North American T-6 Texan or SNJ.

Bunker Hill Naval Air Station was built in Indiana at a site where no previous military aviation facilities had existed. Sailors worked alongside carpenters and machine operators to build barracks, mess facilities, four 5,000-foot runways, a 2,500-foot landing mat, classrooms, repair shops, wooden hangars, warehouses, and storage for 200,000 gallons of aviation gasoline. These facilities would accommodate 6,300 Navy, Coast Guard, and Marine Corps personnel at a cost of $10 million.

Navy recruits, unfamiliar with the location of the base, arrived at farmhouses in the remote section of Miami County to inquire about the way. Several of these lost sailors reported late for duty because area residents, sometimes living only a few miles from the new base, were not sure about its location. Chief P.J. McCarthy is at center in this picture.

The first class of aviation cadets reported to Bunker Hill on September 10, 1943. Seventeen days later, Fredrick Wright, not pictured, was the first to complete a solo flight from the base. By July 1944, a total of 2,802 officers and sailors had received some form of aviation or technical training and had moved into the fighting Navy.

An aviation cadet's day began at 5:30 a.m. Everybody fell out for physical training before breakfast. The limited number of training aircraft made it impossible for everybody to fly at once, so cadets would rotate ground school and the flying schedule between mornings and afternoons. Training often lasted into the darkness.

Ground school incorporated with primary training in the Stearman PT-17 biplane trainer took nine weeks. About 40 percent of candidates washed out before logging the required eight hours of supervised flying time and completing their first solo flight. Intermediate training continued for 11 weeks in the SNV monoplane trainer, where candidates logged another 70 hours before leaving Bunker Hill for advanced training.

Accidents accounted for a majority of noncombat deaths over the course of the war. For every airplane lost in combat in the Pacific theater during 1943, six were lost in accidents. Operational aircraft accidents killed 70 percent of the 15th Army Air Force crews between November 1, 1943, and May 25, 1945.

NAVY SHORE PATROL IN KOKOMO

—Tribune Photo
Men from the Bunker Hill naval air station on Shore Patrol on the streets of Kokomo now are a familiar sight to local citizens. Four of the first "S-P's" assigned to regular duty in Kokomo are shown above.

A 16-year veteran of the Princeton, Indiana, police department before joining the Navy, Floyd Lamar was put in charge of the local shore patrol detail. He was quoted in a *Kokomo Tribune* article saying "Grief? We got plenty of it." Shore patrol and guard duty were rotated among the sailors along with the kitchen, or "mess deck," and the laundry.

A native of Young America, Indiana, Joe Platt played baseball and basketball in high school and was commissioned into the US Navy. Pictured second from right in the second row is Lt. (jg) Joseph M. Platt; he coached the Bunker Hill Bluejackets baseball team to a 54-15 season in 1943. Eighteen years later, Coach Platt brought the Kokomo Wildcats basketball team to the 1961 state championship and was inducted into the Indiana Basketball Hall of Fame in 1974.

While Hoosiers were glad to see the war's end, the deactivation of Bunker Hill Naval Air Station in 1946 ended a relative economic boom in the rural area. The Navy held onto the base but allowed a local committee to manage the land and buildings with hopes of luring industry into the area. The huge indoor swimming pool is fabled to have stored soybeans.

A former Navy maintenance hangar became the Bunker Hill School of Aeronautics in 1947. C.C. Harrah and Howard Pemberton of Michigan hoodwinked Bunker Hill community officials into letting them acquire war surplus property, like this B-24 bomber purchased for $200 from the War Assets Administration, hypothetically to train veterans in the budding aviation industry. The school never hired a faculty or formed a student body. This building burned to the ground in 1956. (Author's collection.)

A 1951 Congressional investigation determined that $5.5 million worth of military surplus materials had been siphoned out of the deactivated Navy base through the Bunker Hill School of Aeronautics. Base commander Harry Curran Jr. was implicated when Julia Mullaney, who worked for Curran's father, was found to be a stockholder in the sham veterans' training program. Congress eventually lost interest in tracking down the stolen war surplus and the whole matter was forgotten. (Courtesy of Craig Trott.)

Two

A Cold War Warms Up

The Cold War was a complex system of nuclear weapons, cloak-and-dagger spies, air defense radar, bombers, air-refueling tankers, fail-safe communications with a pair of red telephones, and alternate command posts with the sole purpose of maintaining an uneasy peace through the threat of massive retaliation, or deterrence. To keep from being attacked, the United States had to build a retaliatory force so inextinguishably powerful that, even after absorbing a devastating first blow, it could deliver a counter-strike of nation-killing proportions. The responsibility of building and maintaining this force of deterrence belonged to the Strategic Air Command (SAC) of the US Air Force. Its motto was "Peace is our Profession."

Such a terrifying prospect was made necessary by the threat of the nuclear-armed Soviet Union. Soviet prime minister Nikita Khrushchev threatened to "bury" the United States, and 20 years later, Pres. Ronald Reagan referred to the Soviets as the "evil empire." Americans well remembered the surprise attack on Pearl Harbor and the near total destruction of Hiroshima by a single atomic bomb, while they stocked fallout shelters and trembled under the sonic booms of nuclear-armed bombers.

Developing the complex weapons systems that were capable of destroying a nation was only half of the equation. Secretary of Defense Robert McNamara once asked rhetorically if the capability would be credible. Would the government of the United States, even if sufficiently provoked, ever consider reducing an entire nation of people into an eerily glowing pile of embers?

For more than 30 years, the men and women stationed at Bunker Hill, later Grissom, Air Force Base nodded somberly to that question. They trained constantly so that they could perform their jobs flawlessly. When they were not training, they were being tested, always cocked, and always ready to stand on the forward wall of the nation's peace.

It was a job they prayed would never be necessary.

The 319th Fighter Interceptor Squadron, 323rd Fighter Bomber Wing, flying F-94 Starfires landed at Bunker Hill Air Force Base in October 1955. During the Korean War, the 319th had earned the distinction of using radar to target and destroy an enemy aircraft. This achievement demonstrated the practicality of the all-weather fighter. A pilot no longer had to see his target in order to kill him. The 319th crest consisted of a tomcat with the slogan "We get ours at night."

Hundreds of pigeons had moved into Hangar No. 7 during the military's absence from Bunker Hill. Workers who were renovating the building neglected to clean the old nests out before starting a welding project and burned the building to the ground in July 1956. Three F-94 aircraft were lost in the fire, but a few months later, Bunker Hill began replacing them with F-89 Scorpions.

The Airways & Air Communication Service (AACS), part of the Military Air Transport Service (now the Air Mobility Command), borrowed a B-47 from SAC to perform high-speed and high-altitude tests of navigation networks, landing systems, and control tower procedures in 1956. Pictured during a visit to Bunker Hill, "Sweet Marie" was returned to bomber duty in 1962 and is currently on static display at Whiteman Air Force Base, Missouri.

The Air Force wasted no time in tearing out the Navy barracks and building these modern lodgings. This aerial photograph was taken of Lancer and Lightning Street looking north. Building No. 300 is in the center of this picture, and construction has begun on the mess hall. Over its lifetime, Building No. 300 would serve as a primary barracks for alert personnel and headquarters for the Office of Special Investigations and the Indiana Wing Civil Air Patrol.

Designated as Hangar No. 200 from the very start, this huge maintenance building was one of the very first construction projects on Bunker Hill. The Navy still owned the base and let all major contracts and supervised construction of the nearly $25 million in new facilities. It was not until 1982 that the Air Force gained the title to the base from the Navy.

The original base post office was located in this building on Kitty Hawk Avenue directly behind the Base Exchange. A new post office was built on the grounds of the former wing supply facility in 1964 between Lancer and Constellation Streets and designated as Building No. 310. Originally a branch of the Peru Post Office, Grissom Air Force Base acquired its own zip code a decade later.

From a very modest beginning, the 305th Civil Engineering Squadron included roads and grounds. Civil engineers train to build and maintain Air Force facilities, including complete combat airfields, and were responsible for much of the renovation at Bunker Hill. William Gentry assumed command of the new 305th Air Refueling Wing in 1970 and razed these buildings as part of his base beautification program.

Building S-334 was built as classrooms for the Naval Reverse Officer Training Corps and was located along what later became Lightning Street, west of the Base Exchange and across the street from the post office. During the 1960s, the Air Force used the building for Boy Scout meetings and then as a thrift store where used furniture and clothing were sold on consignment.

The Air Force used this building south of the gymnasium and swimming pool as the base photography lab. On the northwest corner of Sabre Road and Flyer Street, the structure may have been used by the Navy as a parachute shop.

The ramp was filling up with SAC aircraft during the summer of 1959 as the 305th Bomb Wing began to arrive, and perhaps, as a sign of things to come, the 319th got pushed over to an area near the operations building. Nobody seemed to care though, because they took receipt of the world's fastest fighter, the delta wing F-106, by the first of the next year.

Headquarters for the 305th Bomb Wing was located in this rather shabby Navy surplus building near the west gate. Early maps located the headquarters across the street from the 68th Air Refueling Squadron in the neighborhood of what would later become the nose docks. William Utley was assigned as the deputy commander for maintenance, and William Bowden was assigned as the deputy commander for operations.

The 319th Fighter Interceptor Squadron made its headquarters in this operations building, located along the parking ramp across the street and a little south of the gym and swimming pool. While admitting in the *1961 Base Guide*, which was for newly assigned personnel, that they received support from the 305th Combat Support Group, the 319th Fighter Interceptor Squadron made it very clear that they were "in no way part of the SAC chain of command."

Building S-1 was built in 1959 as headquarters for the 305th Combat Support Group. The 305th Bombardment and Aerial Refueling Wings would call this building home for the next 30 years.

Walter O. Beane commanded the 319th Fighter Interceptor Squadron in 1962 and is shown in the cockpit of one of the wing's newly assigned F-106 Delta Darts. Beane was an experienced fighter pilot who had been shot down over Korea in an F-84 Thunderstreak. Under Beane's command, the 317th Fighter Interceptor Squadron, based at McChord Air Force Base, Washington, won the William Tell Combat Competition in 1958.

Frank O'Brien, pictured in the cockpit of a B-58 Hustler, led the 305th Bomb Wing's move to Indiana. Commissioned in 1939, he was a graduate of the prestigious Navy War College at Newport, Rhode Island. O'Brien was promoted to colonel in 1951 and given command of the 305th Bomb Wing in July 1957. A command pilot with more than 4,500 flying hours, he is the recipient of the Distinguished Flying Cross.

The 305th Bomb Wing's B-47s began to arrive at Bunker Hill Air Force Base in May 1959 even as construction continued on the reactivated and repurposed installation. The 68th Air Refueling Squadron, 4041st Air Base Group was transferred to Bunker Hill in late 1957, claiming the base for the Strategic Air Command.

Neither Bunker Hill nor Grissom, despite tearing down the main gate in 1983 and putting up a visitors' center in its place, were ever particularly welcoming to visitors. Like every SAC base, Bunker Hill was a "closed" installation guarded by heavily armed Air Police.

Beginning its move to Bunker Hill from MacDill Air Force Base, Florida, in the spring of 1959, the 305th Bomb Wing was completely in place and "war ready" by July. The efficiency of the move validated SAC's program of dispersing units to "create a more complex target system for any aggressor," according to Col. Frank O'Brien, commander of the 305th Bomb Wing. The piston engine KC-97 pictured was integrated with the B-47 war plans but proved a poor match for the jet bomber. (Courtesy of the US Air Force.)

The 319th team earned the highest total score of 12 interceptor squadrons during the 1959 William Tell weapons meet. Representing the 30th Air Division at Tyndall Air Force Base, Florida, for the annual Air Defense Command competition, the 319th Fighter Interceptor Squadron also took first place in overall F-89 competition. Pictured are F-106s parked on the ramp. (Courtesy of the US Air Force.)

The 319th returned to Tyndall with its almost-brand-new Mach 2 F-106 fighters in July 1960. During a no-notice scramble, in which the pilots race to get their "cocked" airplanes off the runway, they became the first Air Defense Command unit to have all aircraft score hits on their first pass at a flying drone target. (Courtesy of the US Air Force.)

Building S-13, located west of the original control tower, was constructed by the Navy as Bunker Hill's flight operations center.

Wing Operations in Building S-13 was the center of flying activity where bomber and tanker flight crews did much of their mission planning and received their preflight briefings. Airmen picked up their life support equipment on the way to the flightline and debriefed aircraft maintenance personnel here after their flight.

The original enlisted barracks were assigned by squadron. The first sergeant, who specialized mostly in personnel matters, was responsible for the barracks and everybody who lived there. Most squadrons rotated charge of quarters (CQ) duty among barracks residents. This is Building No. 311 in 1959. (Courtesy of Terry Rasberry.)

Two airmen were typically assigned to each room, and every four men shared a shower and toilet. Later, barracks featured larger rooms with communal showers and dayrooms for socializing. Terry Rasberry is on the right in this picture. (Courtesy of Terry Rasberry.)

The wing commander is responsible for all combat operations on a SAC base while the base commander takes care of everything else. Supervising base security, fire protection, runway maintenance, and even legal contracts, as well as making sure everybody gets fed, are the responsibilities of the base commander. Those functions found their home in Building S-1, headquarters for the 305th Combat Support Group. (Courtesy of Terry Rasberry.)

This photograph was taken during Fire Safety Week in 1960. The base fire department has strung a banner across the road north of base headquarters. This is the southeast corner of Sabre and Liberator Streets on the site of what would become the Air Force Reserve Center 10 years later. Workers in this picture are laying the foundation for the Little White House.

An interesting thing happened on the way to Bunker Hill when an engine fell off the wing of this 305th Bomb Wing B-47. The airplane was able to be repaired, but later, it experienced a couple of career-ending hard landings and is currently on display at the Grissom Air Museum. In July 1960, Bunker Hill was rated 49th among 59 SAC bases for flying safety.

The first stop for all newly assigned personnel in 1959 was the Personnel Processing Center near Sabre and Liberator Streets. The American Red Cross and Family Services shared the building known at the time as S-9. The 434th Air Force Reserve Wing constructed a brick headquarters building west of the site in 1970.

Building S-16, across the street from the original control tower, originally served as the link trainer facility for the Navy. An early flight simulator, the link trainer helped student aviators become familiar with an airplane's control functions. The building was later used as headquarters for the 1915th Airway and Air Communication Squadron, forerunner to the 1915th Communication Squadron, and then functioned as a continuing education classroom.

The 1960 fire department on base included, from left to right, Albert Nagy, Jack Young, George Bartley, Paul Riley, Clair Curtis, Charles Hunter, Robert Smith, James Weedman, Frank Kloss, James Whitehead, Walter Sleeter, John Rogers, Horace Lowe, James Slaughter, James Rogers, John Hudson, Cleveland Tabron, Ronald Legel, Robert Liewellyn, Harold Lemke, Benjamin Duke, Carlton Braden, Victor Wallen, James Edwards, and Thomas Noeveil.

Aircraft, loaded with thousands of pounds of jet fuel, and hundreds of buildings, some of which housed people while others held bombs and bullets, make the base firefighters' job very diverse and challenging. Firefighters train not only to put out fires but also to rescue people from burning airplanes. At Bunker Hill and later Grissom, crash trucks were expected to be on scene, anywhere along the runway, in less than two minutes.

Youth activities were well supported by the organizations at Bunker Hill Air Force Base. In this 1960 photograph, the assistant fire chief Henry Peters is helping these Boy Scouts with their firemanship merit badge. The Scouts are, from left to right, Mike Graham, Randall Summers, John Holland, Danny Manke, Bill Simpson, Dennis Wray, Barry Herbert, and Ken Bentz. The fire department later organized and sponsored Boy Scout Troop No. 369.

The "Little White House" a 36-by-24-foot replica of the one on Pennsylvania Avenue, was constructed by 52 Cass County civic organizations to foster good relations with the Air Force community. Dubbed "Operation Hospitality," the building was displayed in downtown Logansport for one week in 1960 before being moved to Bunker Hill Air Force Base to serve as the family services center. Here, wing commander Frank O'Brien sets the cornerstone in front of the Logan Hotel.

305th Bomb Wing commander Frank O'Brien salutes the flag as it is raised over the Little White House to conclude the dedication ceremony. This particular flag was certified as having flown over the Capitol in Washington on July 4, 1960. It was the first 50-star flag, in recognition of Hawaii, to fly over the Capitol. Logansport mayor Otto Neumann and Forest Spencer, chairman of operation hospitality, are also pictured.

Dedication ceremonies for the Little White House took place in front of the Logan Hotel on September 3, 1960. Logansport mayor Otto Neumann reads the dedication while, from left to right, Audrey Ramsey of family services, base commander Vincent Crane's wife Ruth, wing commander Frank O'Brien, Forest Spencer, and Dick Wolf look on.

It became official in January 1961 when Frank O'Brien revealed his phasing-out program for the wing's B-47s and selected eight flying officers for B-58 training. In eight years, the 305th Bomb Wing had flown its B-47s more than 118,000 flying hours or about 59 million miles. By March, most of the B-47s were gone. (Courtesy of Harold Chatlosh, *Peru Tribune*.)

Shown here in her Convair colors, this B-58 was the first to test drop her mission pod at Mach 2 and was used by NASA in supersonic tests. The airplane was later converted to a training bomber (TB-58) and suffered a crippling cockpit fire in the Grissom nose docks in 1969. The bomber is currently on exhibit at the Grissom Air Museum.

Bunker Hill's first of 39 B-58s were delivered by 305th Bomb Wing commander Frank O'Brien in May 1961. Aptly named "Hoosier Hustler," the bomber was unveiled during Bunker Hill's Armed Forces Day open house and was officially christened by Indiana governor Matthew Welsh. Here, O'Brien is coming down the ladder after his flight from Carswell Air Force Base, Texas.

SAC's rigorous training standards and the high levels of discipline required by the men who worked with nuclear bombs gave rise to the "SAC mentality" and the condition of becoming "SACumcised." From left to right, Sam Wilcox, Vince Faulice, and Al Kanauka of the 305th Bomb Wing happily earned the distinction while training at Carswell in the B-58. (Courtesy of Al Kanuka.)

These Hustler huts were built in the primary-alert area during late 1961 and provided some degree of shelter for the aircraft and the crews who were expected to keep them "cocked" for immediate launch. The last vestiges of Grissom's supersonic bomber were dismantled in the spring of 1970. Many were cut down and reused by the Air National Guard.

Leonard Sullivan became the first 305th Bomb Wing pilot to solo a B-58 from Bunker Hill in November 1961. His crew included John Burch as navigator-bombardier and James Estrada as defense systems operator, all of the 366th Bomb Squadron. Sullivan received his training at Carswell Air Force Base, Texas, right across the runway from the Convair factory. B-58 pilots were later trained in delta winged F-102s at Perrin Air Force Base.

Final phaseout of B-47 bomber wings began in 1963, and the last bombers were out of service by 1965. The very last US Air Force operational aircraft was grounded in 1969. The last recorded flight of a B-47 was on June 17, 1986, to Castle Air Force Base, California, for static display at the Castle Air Museum. These aircraft are in storage at Davis Monthan Air Force Base, Arizona, in 1961. (Courtesy of the US Air Force.)

By 1962, the KC-97, pictured refueling a B-47 bomber, had been proven much too inefficient and was replaced by the jet engined KC-135, a military version of Boeing's 707 airliner. These tankers had been vitally important to worldwide B-47 operations. An example was the support of Arctic reconnaissance flights, where bombers guarded the northern borders against a Communist attack. The last of the KC-97s were given to Air Force Reserve and Air National Guard units and finally phased out completely in 1978. (Courtesy of the US Air Force.)

Cuba's close relationship with the Soviet Union and the presence of Communist-built MIG fighters just 100 miles off the Florida coast led to the Tomcat Squadron's transfer to Homestead Air Force Base, Florida, in March 1963. Now flying F-104s, the 319th was deactivated in December 1969 but then reactivated in July 1971 at Malmstrom Air Force Base, Montana. It was a short run. Flying their old F-106s again, the squadron was shut down for good the following April.

Air Force families found affordable off-base housing and welcoming neighbors in the little town of Bunker Hill. A mostly farming community founded in 1858, Bunker Hill and its Main Street hosted three garages, a hardware store, grocery, post office, and a Methodist church in 1965. Bertie's Tavern is located at the jog in State Road 218, just across the street from the volunteer fire department. (Courtesy of Craig Trott.)

Frank O'Brien recognized aviator Roscoe Turner for his support of strategic airpower during the Cold War. The winner of three Thompson trophies, Turner founded an airline and flight training school at Weir Cook Airport in Indianapolis, training more than 3,500 military pilots during World War II. A B-58 Hustler crew also won the Thompson trophy in 1961, flying a closed 1,000-kilometer course at an average speed of 1,284.73 miles per hour. (Courtesy of Terry Rasberry.)

Operation Greased Lightning was SAC commander Thomas Power's plan for demonstrating the reach and supremacy of the B-58 and the Strategic Air Command in 1963. The global exercise involved three bombers from Bunker Hill and 15 collective refuelings, along with a host of support crews. The crew that made the longest sustained flight in history was awarded the Distinguished Flying Cross in a ceremony at SAC headquarters. The awards were presented by General Powers. (Courtesy of Col. Sid Kubesch.)

On October 16, 1963, the three Bunker Hill B-58s, each consisting of a three-man crew, took off from Anderson Air Force Base Guam at noon and met tankers over Tokyo. From left to right, pilot George Andrews, navigator-bombardier Joseph Guastella, and defense systems operator Clifford Youngblood were among the select crews to make the 8,000-mile sprint from Tokyo to London. (Courtesy of Col. Joseph Guastella.)

From left to right, Sid Kubesch, John Barrett, and Gerard Williamson beat the other two crews when they flew their Hustler on the longest sustained supersonic flight in history. During Operation Greased Lightning, they covered 8,028 miles from Tokyo to London in eight hours, 35 minutes. Even with five inflight refuelings, the flight averaged a scorching 938 miles per hour and demonstrated, particularly to the Communists, the tremendous capability of this nuclear-strike bomber. (Courtesy of Col. Sid Kubesch.)

Burning almost 200 gallons of jet fuel per minute in full afterburner, the success of the Greased Lightning mission depended heavily on the timing and skill required for midair refueling. Kubesch is talking with Gen. Carl "Tooey" Spaatz, the first Air Force chief of staff and largely considered the father of aerial refueling. In 1980, the 305th Air Refueling Wing at Grissom won the prestigious Spaatz Memorial Trophy for its outstanding refueling performance. (Courtesy of Col. Sid Kubesch.)

Operation Greased Lightning pilots flew above 45,000 feet to attain the fastest speed and then dove in on the KC-135 that was waiting more than four miles below. Crews had only been permitted two practice refuelings before the operation and had to devise their own methods to pull up right behind their tankers. This is the view from the boom operator's station in the back of a KC-135.

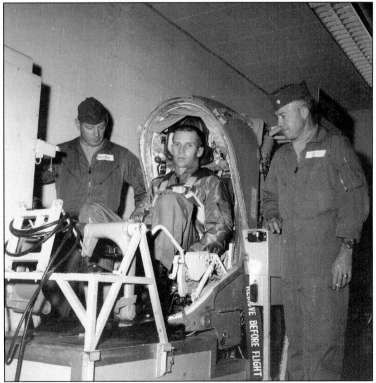

The ejection or escape pod was developed to protect a Hustler crew that had to get out of their 1,400-mile-per-hour airplane at 40,000 feet, where the temperature is 55 below and there is no oxygen. The pod mechanically folded the crewman inside before slamming shut and rocketing out of the airplane. Equipped with parachute, flotation devices, food, and weapons, the pod was unique to the Hustler. (Courtesy of Craig Trott.)

49

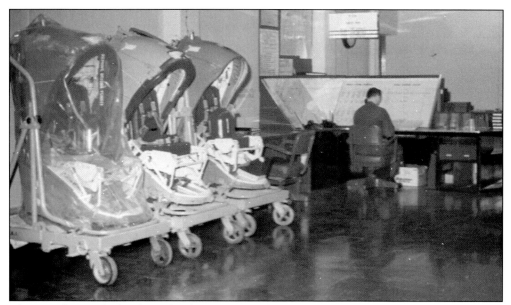

The capsule was the last hope for the airmen in the eleven 305th Hustlers that crashed. Those killed in defense of freedom were John Trevasini, Arthur Freed, Reinardo Moore, William Berry, William Bergdoll, Manuel Cervantes, Richard Blasklee, Floyd Acker, Clarence Lunt, William Bennett, Galen Dultmeier, Ronald Schmidt, Leroy Hanson, Don Close, Eugene Harrington, and Johnny Eubanks. James McElvain was among those saved by the ejection capsule when his B-58 crashed on April 3, 1969, but he was shot down over North Vietnam in 1972 and is presumed dead. (Courtesy of Arley Brewer.)

The Capehart housing program provided for the construction of an additional 365 family housing units on Bunker Hill in 1962. Capehart, formerly Hickam Avenue, is seen at bottom left in this aerial photograph looking north. The housing gate is at the top along Indiana State Road 218.

Pres. Lyndon Johnson and Lady Bird Johnson made a brief stop at Bunker Hill on their way from South Bend to Pittsburgh in April 1964 and ended up shaking hands with an enthusiastic crowd. Lady Bird Johnson handed out roses from a bouquet that had been presented to her by the wife of wing commander Paul Carlton, Helen Carlton. Traveling with the president were state senators Vance Hartke and Birch Bayh and Indiana governor Matthew Welsh. (Courtesy of 305th Wing Historian.)

Before boarding Air Force One, wing commander Paul Carlton made sure to remind the president who had commanded the longest sustained supersonic flight in history, which was the crew of the Greased Lightning Operation. The crew members of that mission have formed up in front of the boarding ladder and are being introduced to the First Lady by Helen Carlton. (Courtesy of Col. Sid Kubesch.)

To make things easier for Bunker Hill families, the Air Force built Randall Elementary School. Part of the Maconaquah School Corporation, most Bunker Hill and Grissom kids can proudly call themselves Braves.

The delta wing Hustler landed in a nose-high attitude, making it impossible for the pilot to see the runway ahead. Jack Strank, who did not break this bomber, used his pitot tube on the nose to stay lined up. "If I couldn't see concrete alongside I knew to steer in the other direction." It took a lot of practice to get it right.

HH-43 "Huskie" helicopters provided Bunker Hill with an extended rescue capability in 1965. The downwash from the rescue helicopter rotors pushed heat and flames back to allow rescuers access to a fire-stranded aircrew. These helicopters typically carried a fire suppression kit, seen at right, and were assigned to Detachment 17 of the Central Air Rescue Service. (Courtesy of the US Air Force.)

The Cold War had budgeted the Strategic Air Command into the largest organization in the US Air Force. By the end of 1964, SAC had assigned 4,400 airmen to Bunker Hill Air Force Base with a monthly payroll of almost $1 million going off base to the local economy. While this figure does not include local Air Force contracts, it amounts to $7,590,000 in 2015 dollars. (Courtesy of Craig Trott.)

Even allowing for all the cutting-edge technology that was engineered into the Hustler, the airplane's spindly nose gear caused the most problems. To fit the landing gear inside the sleek wings and fuselage, the tires were small and were supported by steel wheels in the likely event of a blowout. This airplane was repaired and later flown to Davis-Monthan with the rest of the Hustler fleet in December 1969.

One of the first Mercury astronauts, Air Force lieutenant colonel Virgil "Gus" Grissom (left), for whom this base was renamed in 1968, visited Bunker Hill Air Force Base and caught up with his old friend Larry Duval. The two are standing in front of an F-102, which was not based at Bunker Hill, but was used to teach new B-58 pilots the idiosyncrasies of flying delta wing aircraft. In 1965, Duval became the first 305th pilot to fly the B-58 1,000 hours. (Courtesy of Craig Trott.)

General Electric J-79 engines were kept on hand at Bunker Hill in 1966 to maintain the 305th Bomb Wing's state of readiness. During a Bar None operational readiness exercise, engines were replaced on two B-58s in a quick 90 minutes. "The crews were motivated. The airplane was needed to relieve other aircraft from alert duty," said the noncommissioned officer in charge, Charles Fritz, of the engine conditioning section to *The Hustler*. (Courtesy of Arley Brewer.)

A highly complex aircraft, the B-58 required considerable maintenance, much of which required specialized equipment and ground personnel. In 1969, Maj. Gen. Sherman Martin told the Air Force chief of staff that SAC could maintain and operate six B-52 wings for the price of the two B-58 wings. These figures have long been disputed by Col. George Holt, who worked in the Strategic Forces Plan Division at the Pentagon. This photograph was taken in 1966. (Courtesy of Arley Brewer.)

During aerial refueling, a leaking refueling boom and a cold winter night coated Alan Dugard's windshield with a thick coat of ice over southern Indiana. Relying strictly on the boom operator's instructions, he was able to stay with the tanker and complete the refueling. It was not until he dropped below the tanker and thawed the ice that he noticed part of the boom still stuck in the nose of his airplane. Dugard and his crew brought the B-58 back to Bunker Hill safely.

The 305th Organizational Maintenance Squadron is responsible for making sure that its aircraft can launch. Maintenance teams usually show up six hours before a flight to complete a checklist with the crew chief and flight crew where everybody will verify that any problems with the airplane have been repaired. A team then is on hand again to recover the aircraft when it lands, working closely with the crew chief to resolve any maintenance problems. (Courtesy of Arley Brewer.)

Displaying three of the 44 trophies won by the 305th Bomb Wing at the 1965 SAC Bombing and Navigation Competition are, from left to right, William Hill, who commanded the 366 Bomb Squadron; Louis Chenger, of Organizational Maintenance; and Thomas Chaffee, of Armament Electronics. The B-58 Greased Lightning that represented the 305th in the competition is the same aircraft that claimed the international speed record in 1963.

Miss Indiana Jane Rutledge visited Bunker Hill Air Force Base in August 1966 and was allowed a close inspection of the record-breaking Greased Lightning. The bomber would soon be deployed to Fairchild Air Force Base to compete against other bomb wings in SAC's annual combat competition. Crew members navigator-bombardier Don Itzen (left) and aircraft commander Mackie Sorrell (right) are her hosts.

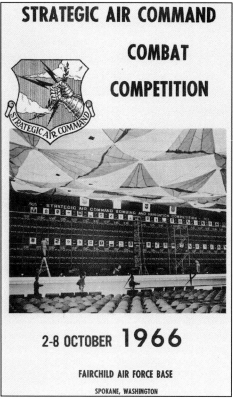

STRATEGIC AIR COMMAND

COMBAT

COMPETITION

2-8 OCTOBER 1966

FAIRCHILD AIR FORCE BASE

SPOKANE, WASHINGTON

SAC assigned its small B-58 fleet to only two wings, the 305th Bomb Wing at Bunker Hill and the 43rd Bomb Wing at Little Rock Air Force Base near Jacksonville, Arkansas. In anticipation of the annual SAC Bombing and Navigation Competition, the Jacksonville Chamber of Commerce challenged the Bunker Hill Community Council that "our bomber can beat your bomber" and anted up a razorback hog. The Bunker Hill flight crew may have provoked some side bets when they suited up like Indianapolis race car drivers.

The SAC Bombing and Navigation Competition grew in size and complexity between 1949 and 1992, spawning several other competitions like navigation, aerial refueling, and munitions loading. From its earliest years through 1992, its last year, the competition was conducted to build morale, sharpen skills, and test crews' abilities and equipment under a demanding environment. The 305th, which had won most of the B-58 competitions in 1965, placed 10th in 1966, but defeated the Little Rock team, which finished in 13th place.

The 305th Organizational Maintenance Squadron's inspection branch was responsible for the periodic phase inspections of the wing's bombers and other aircraft. These inspections typically take several days, as every nut and every clamp is tightened, every service panel is inspected for leaks from nose to tail, and specialists from other squadrons are called in to make necessary repairs. (Courtesy of Arley Brewer.)

Isaiah 6:8 inspired one of the memorial stained-glass windows in the SAC chapel at Offutt AFB in Nebraska. It reads, "Then I heard the voice of the Lord saying, 'Whom shall I send? And who will go for us?' And I said, 'Here am I. Send me!' " The base chapel at Bunker Hill was located conveniently in the middle of the enlisted dorms offering Protestant services and a Catholic Mass in 1966.

The B-58 was a tank of jet fuel with wings. Carrying almost 14,000 gallons in its four main tanks, the airplane's center of gravity could be maintained automatically by moving fuel from the forward to aft tanks. But without a centerline mission pod attached to the underbelly of the bomber, a nose counterweight was needed to keep the airplane on its feet.

CRASH OF THE B-58 "HUSTLER"

At the height of the Cold War, on the night of Dec. 12, 1966, the residents of McKinney were startled by the sound of an explosion. Many locals converged on this hill to find a large fiery crater, and the wreckage of an Air Force B-58. All three crew members perished. Official cause never released to public. Over

Given by friends, family, & citizens of Lincoln Co.

Operation Bullseye was conducted on the range at Elgin Air Force Base, Florida, to test the feasibility of using the B-58 for low-altitude bombing in Vietnam. On December 12, 1966, Richard Blakeslee was conducting a low-level navigation run, flying about 550 miles per hour 400 feet above the ground, when he crashed near McKinney, Kentucky. The entire crew, including Floyd Acker and Clarence Lunt, was killed.

Air Force lieutenant colonel Gus Grissom was a Hoosier boy. Born in Mitchell, Indiana, and educated at Purdue, Grissom flew 190 combat missions in Korea. As one of the first Mercury astronauts, he completed two successful space missions and then was killed on January 27, 1967, while training for an Apollo mission at Cape Kennedy, Florida.

Grissom Air Force Base was renamed in the astronaut's honor on May 12, 1968. An open house, which included an aerial demonstration performed by the US Air Force Thunderbirds, was held in conjunction with the dedication ceremony.

An estimated crowd of 48,000 helped to dedicate the new Grissom Air Force Base, touring the static aircraft displays and witnessing a parachuting exhibition of the Army Golden Knights. Colonel Grissom's parents, widow, two sons, brothers, and sister, along with fellow astronaut Gordon Cooper, attended the dedication. Besides this KC-135, Grissom hosted an assortment of visiting military aircraft throughout the day.

Bunker Hill Air Force Base included an assortment of weapons and weapons systems that were critical to the SAC mission. Protection of these vital resources was the responsibility of the security police and their Military Working Dog Section. A dog handler is using another security policeman to demonstrate his animal's capabilities during the base open house in 1968. The Air Police became the Air Force Security Police in 1966, a title that better defined its role of protecting Air Force personnel and resources.

Three

SURROGATE WARS

Despite all the fanfare, Air Force headquarters decided that the Hustler was just not the right airplane at the right time. Never mind a series of low-altitude tests SAC conducted successfully with the B-58 in 1959 and 1962, advances in Soviet surface-to-air missile technology left the bomber vulnerable in the high-altitude envelope where it had been designed to perform its mission.

Col. George Holt, USAF (Ret.), was assigned to the Pentagon in 1969 and studied the cost and effectiveness of the B-58 as compared to other weapons systems. Admitting a bias stemming from his assignment as a B-58 navigator-bombardier at Bunker Hill, Holt argues that SAC skewed its numbers to justify trading its Hustler fleet in order to keep four B-52 wings. His research demonstrates that when comparing airplane to airplane, the Hustler was cheaper to own, faster to get in the air, and more likely to evade Soviet air defenses and reach its targets than the B-52. But the decision to scrap the Hustlers was made by cost-conscious politicians influenced by Secretary of Defense Robert McNamara to believe that intercontinental ballistic missiles (ICBMs) had rendered the manned bomber force obsolete.

The newly designated 305th Aerial Refueling Wing at Grissom became the largest of its kind in the Air Force. SAC was the primary manager for the tanker fleet, and 305th crews had been rotating in and out of Thailand and Guam in support of combat missions over Vietnam since 1967. The program ran through the Christmas Bombings of 1972 when the North Vietnamese came back to the peace talks and agreed to release US prisoners of war.

When Bakalar Air Force Base near Columbus, Indiana, was closed in 1970, the 434th Special Operations Wing, a reserve unit that had flown 6,251 combat hours in Vietnam, came to Grissom. The 930th Tactical Air Group brought with it 31 A-37B ground-attack fighters, while the 931st came with six older A-37As, a C-123 transport, and 17 battle-worn fighters from South Vietnam.

The ramp was full once again.

TB-58 663, which is currently on display in the Grissom Air Museum, was severely damaged in 1969 when an electrical fire destroyed the cockpit. The useless bomber was stored in Nose Dock No. 4 before being polished and placed on display with other historic aircraft near the main gate. With the mission pod drained and engines removed, the airplane would have fallen on its tail if the navigator's position had not first been filled with concrete.

Sid Kubesch was able to welcome an old friend to Nebraska in December 1969. While he was assigned to SAC headquarters, his famous B-58, now permanently named *Greased Lightning* after the record-setting mission, flew for the very last time from Grissom to Offutt Air Force Base. Jerry Anderson, Norman Menke, and Leonard Fross made the last flight. The *Greased Lightning* is now on display at the Strategic Air and Space Museum near Ashland, Nebraska.

The Pentagon had decided in 1965 that the B-58 was too expensive and would be gone by 1971. Among the many explanations offered was that the small number of aircraft "entails a greater expense per vehicle than a large force because of the peculiar [needs]." But the Hustler had been successful in demonstrating SAC's capabilities and deterring the possibility of nuclear war. This Grissom bomber was placed into storage in 1969 and scrapped in 1977.

The last of the Hustlers departed Grissom on January 16, 1970, for storage at Davis-Monthan Air Force Base near Tucson. Franklin R. Ewan was at the controls for this final flight. By 1977, all but nine of the 116 Hustlers had been scrapped. During this same week, 600 Air Force reservists of the 931st Tactical Support Group from Bakalar Air Force Base in Columbus, Indiana, reported to Grissom.

Crews and aircraft from Bunker Hill and Grissom rotated in and out of U-Tapao Air Base, Thailand, from 1967 until 1973. Tankers from the 305th supported the Arc Light missions with targets including enemy infiltration along the Ho Chi Min Trail in Laos and Cambodia and the Linebacker missions of the 1970s in North Vietnam. These thirsty and bomb-laden F-105s need fuel to reach their targets "up North." (Courtesy of the US Air Force.)

The Looking Glass mission was originally tested in the early 1960s as part of SAC's Post Attack Command Control System. Specially modified EC-135As, like the one on the right in this picture, designated by the "white top," were airborne around the clock and capable of assuming command of SAC's mission in the event that its headquarters in Nebraska was attacked and destroyed. The other aircraft are KC-135(R) models.

With the introduction of the E4A, a military version of Boeing's 747, as the National Emergency Airborne Command Post (NEACP), the 305th Air Refueling Wing, and later the 70th Air Refueling Squadron, assumed responsibility for the Looking Glass mission in April 1970. EC-135 aircraft crewed by Grissom's 305th Avionics Maintenance Squadron and the 1915th Communications Squadron remained on airborne alert around the clock to provide communications between NEACP and the SAC network.

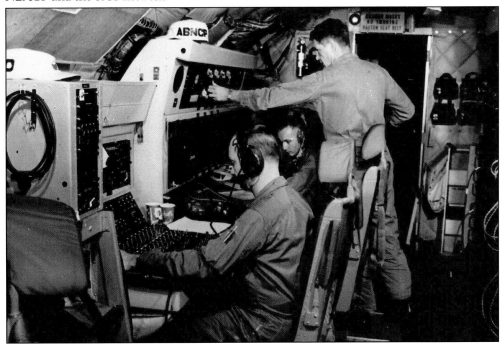

During a typical Looking Glass mission, the aircraft runs a link between the airborne command post and other Post-Attack Command and Control System (PACCS) aircraft from Grissom. This multifaceted chain of communication ensures that, in the event the United States were attacked, SAC's bombers and missiles are no farther away than the White House telephone. The last continuous Looking Glass mission was performed by Grissom crews on July 24, 1990.

NEACP aircraft came to Grissom in 1983 with their own complement of security police. Based out of SAC headquarters at Offutt Air Force Base, Nebraska, the E-4 staged out of several SAC bases in what former Grissom pilot Max Jordan called a "shell game" intended to keep the Soviets guessing. (Courtesy of the US Air Force.)

Former 305th Security Police Squadron member Elgin Shaw said, "A bomb dog team and spotter would always sweep the NEACP facility, parking apron and any associated equipment to be hooked up to the AC. . . . this just prior to the AC being wheels down." Grissom security police were responsible for the aircraft and crew as long as they were on the base.

As many as 400 Reserve Officer Training Corps (ROTC) cadets trained at Bunker Hill and Grissom every summer through much of the 1960s and 1970s. Two four-week programs provided cadets with experience in every operational aspect of the SAC mission. Between the marching, room inspections, and familiarization flights, cadets experienced the rugged challenge of an abbreviated jungle survival school. In 1971, this cadet has fashioned a shelter from his parachute.

Before an airman could try to survive in the jungle, he would first need to get out of his parachute harness. This phase of the training, held at Frances Slocum Forest Reserve on the banks of the Mississinewa River, teaches cadets what to do if their parachute is snagged in a tree. Over the years, the training was expanded from basic survival skills to include how to evade a pursuing enemy and how to survive captivity.

The added threat of Soviet sea-launched ballistic missiles considerably narrowed the 15-minute warning that SAC considered essential for the survivability of its deterrent force. In 1971, SAC moved part of its 70 FB-111s from costal bases inland. Six nuclear-armed bombers from the 715th Bomb Squadron at Pease Air Force Base, New Hampshire, rotated through Grissom in pairs along with a 200-airman support detachment. (Courtesy of Craig Trott.)

Kokomo High School alumnus William Gentry returned to Indiana as commander of the new 305th Air Refueling Wing during the mission transition in 1970. The next year, he was in the alert area to welcome FB-111 crews from Pease Air Force Base. The Quonset-style hangars in the background were built specifically for the two visiting bombers, which were loaded with their nuclear weapons only after landing and being placed into alert, combat-ready status. (Courtesy of Craig Trott.)

The 434th Special Operations Wing at Grissom began flying the A-37 Dragonfly in 1971. Heavily modified from the trainer model, the counterinsurgency and close air support bomber had more powerful engines and an aerial refueling capability. Aircrews of the 930th and 931st Tactical Fighter Wings often used Camp Atterbury for gunnery practice and Grissom tankers for gas.

Flying F-4 Phantoms, the US Air Force Aerial Demonstration Squadron, known as the Thunderbirds, practice for an air show at Grissom in September 1971. Created in 1953 to represent the US Air Force around the world, the Thunderbirds are assigned to the 57th Wing and are based at Nellis AFB, Nevada. (Courtesy of Craig Trott.)

Catch-22 is a 1970 dark comedy novel by Joseph Heller about the Air Force during World War II. The cast of the movie adaptation included a star-studded collection of 18 World War II–vintage B-25 bombers. One of these, *Passionate Paulette*, tail No. 44-29939, made her last flight to Grissom in April 1972.

Passionate Paulette is among 15 *Catch 22* bombers that remain intact. After her arrival at Grissom, she was ceremoniously towed out to Sabre Street and placed on static display with several other historic aircraft. The display welcomed visitors to Grissom for many years, and *Passionate Paulette*, now without her sassy nose art, is currently on display at the Grissom Air Museum.

Cliff Crowe, president of the Grissom Community Council and manager of JC Penney in Kokomo, participates in a ceremonial groundbreaking for the new Alert Visitation Center in October 1973. The communities of Peru, Kokomo, and Logansport had each contributed $5,000 toward providing a place where alert crews could visit their families. Also pictured is civil engineer Garry Dressel. The ceremony was attended by supportive community and business leaders from throughout the three-county region.

Promoted to brigadier general in 1979, Lyman "Gene" Buzard earned his commission and pilot wings through the Aviation Cadet Program and flew an impressive 9,500 hours during his career with SAC. He commanded first the 305th Combat Support Group and then the Air Refueling Wing from 1974 until 1977. Congressman "Bud" Hillis, waiting with speech in hand, provided tremendous budget support for Grissom from 1971 until 1987.

Anno Marie Huschle has the unique distinction of being the last baby scheduled to be born at Grissom's base hospital on June 15, 1973. President Nixon ended the military draft in January, and the armed forces just did not have enough doctors to go around. Hospital commander Dr. J.B. Johnson closed the OB-GYN clinic and adjusted other services after losing several medical professionals from his staff.

The flight crew representing the 305th Air Refueling Wing at the SAC Bombing and Navigation Competition in 1974 consisted of, from left to right, boom operator Winford Barnes, aircraft commander Carl Pampe, copilot David Kinzer, and navigator Ken Thomas. The "Hoosier Hotshots" nose art was hand painted on the aircraft by Joan McLeod, whose husband was assigned to the 70th Air Refueling Squadron. (Courtesy of Craig Trott.)

A select team from the 305th Field Maintenance Squadron was recognized as "Best KC-135 Support Team at the 1974 SAC Bombing and Navigation Competition. Pictured are, from left to right, (kneeling) John Conway, Paul Allen, Delbert Verhest, Gerald Miller, Randal Pruesser, Daniel Varney, and Paul Jach; (standing) Charles Curtis, Joshua Stewart, Russell Freidman, Jimmy Jeffreys, Lonnie Jenkins, Wayne Lerner, and Delrod McClammy. (Courtesy of Craig Trott.)

Miss 500 Festival queen Andrea McCall (far left) attended the 1974 SAC Bombing and Navigation Competition at Barksdale AFB, Louisiana, as a guest of the 305th. The space suit in the wing's display booth was worn by Gus Grissom while he was training for the successful 1965 Gemini 3 flight aboard the *Molly Brown*. (Courtesy of Craig Trott.)

A lightweight sidearm was required by airmen who had to jump out of crippled airplanes and might find themselves in the midst of unfriendly company. Much lighter than the .45-caliber pistol used by the other branches of the Armed Forces, the Air Force adopted the Smith & Wesson Model 15 in 1962. The combat masterpiece remained the standard sidearm until the Air Force adopted NATO-approved Berettas in 1992.

Air Force women were a Grissom novelty in 1975 when Ginny Zapata Kelley was assigned as the security police desk sergeant. Women were first permitted to join the Air Force in 1948, and in 1967, grade restrictions were lifted, permitting women to serve in supervisory and command positions. The first women were admitted to the Air Force Academy and accepted for pilot training in 1976. Today's Air Force is 30 percent female. (Courtesy of Annie Robb.)

Women in the Air Force were prohibited from serving in combat-related fields in 1977, but security police personnel of both genders were responsible for the defense of Grissom. 305th Security Police Squadron law enforcement specialist Debbie Anspach trains with an M-203 grenade launcher at Camp Atterbury near Columbus, Indiana. Grissom security police used the camp for their annual air base ground-defense training. (Courtesy of Debbie Anspach.)

SAC reversed a previous directive in May 1979 and permitted the return of the distinctive "Checkerboard" tail fins to the 305th Air Refueling Wing's KC-135s. While the Field Maintenance Squadron was repainting the tail, wing commander Richard Wallace said the "checkerboard signifies that this is a winning wing." This Grissom tanker was photographed during a visit to March Air Force Base, California, in 1985.

The 3rd Airborne Command and Control Squadron flew its last mission in December 1975. The squadron was organized at Grissom in 1970 as part of a worldwide command and control network. Its primary mission was to provide a survivable airborne radio relay between the president and SAC headquarters. Among the crew aboard the last flight was James Spence, who made Air Force history in 1975 by becoming one of the first navigators to command a flying unit.

SAC commander general Russell Dougherty presented the 305th wing commander Jerome Barnes with the Charles Trail Logistics Award in 1976. Topping every other base in SAC, the 305th was judged excellent in overall areas of maintenance, supply, transportation, and munitions. The wing was recognized as an outstanding unit in 1974 and also won the Staff Sergeant Richard Rousher Trophy as the best tanker unit in the 8th Air Force.

Gen. Curtis LeMay's World War II campaigns, his "SAC Doctrine," and his disagreements with Presidents Kennedy and Johnson over the Bay of Pigs and the Vietnam War while serving as Air Force chief of staff left a formidable, controversial, and enduring legacy, especially on the Strategic Air Command. In 1977, the retired general attended a 305th Wing Anniversary "dining-in" and is welcomed to Grissom's Officer's Club by security policeman Dwight Jones. This photograph was taken by Don Baxter. (Courtesy of Anthony Trzeciak.)

A late January blizzard all but shut down Grissom Air Force Base in 1978. Typically, mission essential personnel were required to report for duty and found themselves stranded on the base. US 31 and State Road 218 were completely closed from the nearly 25 inches of snow that fell on north-central Indiana. Runways and aircraft alert areas enjoyed a priority for snow removal crews, but civil engineers had all the major thoroughfares on base open a day after the storms.

More sociable and diverse patrol dogs had replaced the sentry dogs by 1978. Working with their security police handler, the dogs patrol secure areas on base during the hours of darkness. Because of the animals' keen senses, a single K-9 patrol was just as effective as three security policemen. Special purpose dogs perform a variety of unique tasks, like drug and bomb detection.

Few aircraft were equipped with radios when the Navy built the original control tower at Bunker Hill during World War II, and student pilots often relied on hand or flag signals from the tower. Technology had improved by the time the Air Force started using the tower, which has been replaced twice. When this picture was taken in the 1970s, the tower had become base operations, and a snack bar was added for convenience.

Grissom's 45th Tactical Fighter Squadron, a component of the 434th Tactical Fighter Wing, replaced its fleet of 24 A-37 Dragonflies with 28 A-10 Thunderbolt II aircraft between 1980 and 1981. The upgrade was part of the Air Force's continuing effort to enhance the reserve components and further complement active duty wings in accordance with the "total force" policy. The A-37 pictured here was assigned to the 71st Special Operations Squadron at Grissom in 1971. (Courtesy of the US Air Force.)

The 1982 open house offered dissident groups a platform to protest against the buildup of nuclear arms in Europe. Soviets turned up the heat in the Cold War with their plan to position nuclear-armed SS-20 ground-launched missiles within striking distance of Western Europe. NATO and President Reagan countered the move with Pershing II ground-launched cruise missiles pointed back at the Soviets. These protestors were quietly escorted off base by the Air Force Security Police.

A giant C-5 Galaxy drew the largest crowd at Grissom's June 1982 open house. A crowd of about 15,000 visited the base to see a static display of several visiting aircraft. Without an aerial demonstration, several airmen, including Gary Church, of security police; Jeff Ross, of fuels distribution; Kathy Ingersoll, of services squadron; and Randy Naylor, of public affairs; entertained visitors with their musical and magic talents.

Following several fatal traffic accidents on US 31 outside the main gate, US representative Bud Hillis helped obtain funding for an access ramp off the highway in 1980. The new ramp allowed motorists to enter the base from the north without having to stop for the traffic light. In 1983, the main gate, which had controlled entry for almost 30 years, was replaced by a friendlier visitors' center.

The 45th Fighter Squadron members seen here include pilots, life support, ops support, intel, and medical support in 1992. Among those pictured are Curt Girton, Craig Hunsberger, Morris Bromfield, Glen Robinson, Duane Riddle, Mark Lampe, Andy Anderson, Don Windt, Brian Holland, Dale Gaunt, Kurt Rauscher, Mark Pozycki, Chris Andrews, JC Davis, Frank Countryman, Ozzie Gorbitz, Kevin Calhan, Andy Duffin, Dan Hamill, Mat Heuss, John Miller, Rick Maughmer, Dave Anewalt, Chuck Dobias, TJ Ropp, Chris Fesler, Maureen McAllen, Dale Inman, Ward Motz, Bob Gold, Mike Gliechman, Dennis Lipp, Ron Miller, Mike Bruno, Sonya Brown, Jimmie Stewart, Gerry Werth, Wayne Burton, Mike Spurlock, Dan Brown, Dennis Hughes, Dick Scherer, Dennis Redding, Phil Shott, and Harold Morgan. (Courtesy of Tim Cahoon.)

The 45th Tactical Fighter Squadron's A-10 in the foreground on the taxiway was capable of carrying a variety of ordinance including 1,350 rounds of tank-killing 30mm cannon ammunition and 16,000 pounds of bombs and missiles. The aircraft can loiter near battle areas at low air speeds for extended periods of time and operate in low-ceiling and low-visibility conditions.

The 434th Tactical Fighter Wing's A-10 pilots and maintenance crews from the 930th Consolidated Aircraft Maintenance Squadron won the annual "Gunsmoke II" gunnery competition at Nellis Air Force Base, Nevada. Grissom crews scored best in strafing runs, low-angle bombing, and weapons loading against six other units from Tactical Air Command bases in 17 states. While these A-10s taxi, the NEACP E-4 is parked in the background.

When necessary runway renovations temporarily closed Grissom's airfield, mission essential aircraft and personnel moved to the Indianapolis International Airport. Paul Daugherty is guarding Air Force One in Indianapolis during a visit by President Reagan.

Jim Frankenfield, a SAC Master Technician, is presented with the "Busted Knuckles" award by the deputy commander of maintenance. The annual Air Force–wide event recognizes the maintenance career field's top performers based on their aircraft capabilities. Frankenfield said, "The people at Grissom represented the Air Force core values Integrity first, Service before self and Excellence in all we do, before it was recognized as the Air Force way."

The KC and EC-135 Stratotankers require periodic phase inspections to insure that all of the systems are performing and to check for regular wear and tear. These nose docks allow technicians to work on the big airplanes in a more controlled environment away from Indiana's numbing winter winds and scorching summer sun.

Duane Gordon, center, represented the 305th Security Police Squadron at the Indianapolis Motor Speedway for an Armed Forces Day celebration in 1982. Since 1978, the speedway has honored all branches of the US military on Armed Forces Day weekend, including an oath of enlistment ceremony for new recruits. This traditional preamble is read before each Memorial Day race: "On this Memorial Day weekend, we pause in a moment of silence, to pay homage to those individuals who have given their lives—unselfishly, and unafraid—so that we may witness as free men and women, the world's greatest sporting event." (Courtesy of Duane Gordon.)

The enlisted barracks remained the same six community latrines shared by two men to a room until the antimilitary perceptions of post-Vietnam turned the latrines into showers and the barracks into dormitories. Remodeling began in 1983 when bathrooms were built between two rooms and the exterior got a complete facelift. Room refrigerators and wall-to-wall carpeting contribute to the luxuries of the "unaccompanied enlisted dorms." The new dining (mess) hall is at the top of this picture.

Life support is about more than giving a pilot a parachute and an enthusiastic thumbs up. The Air Force–wide Wild Stallion Combat Survival, Search, and Rescue training was founded in 1984 by 45th Tactical Fighter Squadron (TFS) life support technician Dan Brown, on the right, with Denny Redding and Ben James. Aircrew life support has a mandatory directive to teach survival skills, and Wild Stallion provides uniform training, which can then be taken back to squadrons by course graduates. (Courtesy of Tim Cahoon.)

A crew chief and assistant crew chief from the 305th Organizational Maintenance Squadron meet their KC-135 during a deployment to March Air Force Base, California, in 1985. This is their airplane. Their names are painted on the side of the fuselage, and they have to know every inch of it, inside and out. 70th Air Refueling Squadron commander Gary Schuck said in 1983, "A good crew chief is priceless. He's got to be the sole person who knows all about his aircraft."

This Grissom tanker of the 434th Air Refueling Wing has been modified with more powerful, fuel-efficient engines to become a KC-135(R) model. Replacing the A models of the 1950s, the Rs came with self-starting engines, which did not require auxiliary power carts; antiskid brakes; and an upgraded instrument panel. SAC began the modifications in 1985, and the airplanes are easily recognized by the larger engines and taller horizontal stabilizer.

The massive maintenance building known as Hangar No. 200 could easily shelter up to four KC-135s with their 130-foot wingspan and 42-foot tail fin. The nose docks and the Consolidated Base Personnel Office can be seen at the top.

Only the annual Snow Parade, a prewinter inspection of the civil engineers' snow removal equipment, could bring Santa out to the line. Trucks, tractors, and plows have been lined up with military precision outside Hangar No. 200 and almost underneath the tail of a reserve KC-135. At the parade, wing staff personnel did inspections, and engineers showed off their inventory of giant snow blowers and plows used to keep the runways clear.

This Grissom KC-135 is touching down at Howard Air Force Base. Throughout the 1980s, the 305th Air Refuelling Wing (ARW) Detachment 1, Howard Air Force Base, Panama, supported the 1st Special Operations Wing. The unit's résumé includes drug interdiction efforts between 1983 and 1985. From October to November 1983, it supported the rescue of US nationals from Cuban invaders in Grenada, and in 1989, it participated in the restoration of democracy to Panama during Operation Just Cause.

Sharon Kehrer Michaels said about her deployment with the 305th to Howard Air Force Base: "There was nothing romantic (about Panama) except the love of a memory of doing a good job with great people. The people there worked hard and played hard, but we always met the mission. The support of 1st SOW was primary, without the 135 and the people who worked there, the operation would never have enjoyed the success we achieved."

Grissom airmen Thomas McDerby, 29, of New Jersey; John Bristow, 25, of Illinois; Wayne Ching, 25, of Hawaii; and Quinn DeWitt, 31, of Indiana, were all killed in June 1986 when their KC-135 crashed into the jungle outside Howard Air Force Base. The crew were returning from a nighttime refueling mission when their tanker was damaged during a hard landing. These are a few of the 305th airmen who never returned home.

Visitors were permitted a close inspection of a T-37 during the 1987 open house. A trainer version of the A-37 ground-attack fighters that were based at Grissom in the 1970s, these airplanes belonged to the 71st Flying Training Wing and were used in the Accelerated Copilot Enrichment Program. Much cheaper to fly than a KC-135, these military versions of a Cessna 310 allowed copilots to gain flying experience.

Competing in the 1987 SAC Bombing and Navigation Competition was crew E-110R of the 305th Air Refuelling Squadron (AREFS). Sporting a moustache, aircraft commander Ron Zeimmer is kneeling on the far right. Kneeling on the far left is boom operator Ricky Dayton, and next to him is copilot Chuck Jones. Spare navigator "Cali" Garcia is standing on the far left. Jeff Johnson, who was the crew's assigned navigator, is standing on the far right. Vital to the aircrew's success was the maintenance and ground support team who are also pictured. (Courtesy of Max Jordan.)

During Desert Shield and Desert Storm, KC-135R tankers from Grissom's 434th supported combat missions over Iraq. In 1982, a KC-135, not pictured, crewed by Smokey Rickard, Vincent Guida, John Salmon, and Mike Harrison, became the first Air Force crew to be refueled from a freshly modified R model. The refueling mission was a test, and SAC committed to a complete fleet conversion in 1985.

Air traffic control is just one of the many and varied duties performed by the 1915th Communications Squadron. While the tower people are the most visible, radar approach controllers work in darkened rooms to handle overflights and traffic from Logansport to Marion. Maintaining the "reins of command" at Grissom involves technicians in a wide spectrum of communications support from repairing a speaker to alignment of precision approach control radar.

Naval aviator Bob Wirt parked his supersonic F-18 Hornet on the same ramp that once held biwinged Navy trainers. While the Air Force people who fly airplanes are called pilots, the US Navy refers to them as aviators. Perhaps this is to distinguish them from the more traditional maritime Navy, where sailors pilot boats. Wirt began his military career as an Air Force ROTC cadet at Purdue University. (Courtesy of Tim Cahoon.)

Just like Disneyland, a line of young pilots has formed to sit in a replica T-38 Talon. The Air Force Thunderbirds were demonstrating their capability of airpower with the Talon in 1987, and the Air Force Recruiting Service brought this very popular display to Grissom's open house. Hangar No. 200 is in the background.

The 45th Tactical Fighter Squadron put on a demonstration of its A-10s' capabilities during the 1988 open house. In a carefully choreographed performance, munitions specialists detonated explosives of varying magnitude along the runway to simulate bomb and strafing runs while the A-10 swooped overhead. Because the A-10 performance made more noise than the famous Air Force Thunderbirds who followed them, the local pilots stole the show. (Courtesy of Tim Cahoon.)

The tradition of the fini-flight, designed to accompany milestones in the career of an individual or an entire crew, is believed to have originated during World War II. The ritual was officially first noted during the Vietnam War, when an aircrew celebrated a safe completion of 100 combat missions by dousing each other with beer. Today, a fini-flight is usually a separate event in recognition of an individual's or aircrew's notable contribution to the US Air Force. (Courtesy of Tim Cahoon.)

From August 1990 to June 1991, aircraft and personnel of the 305th ARW deployed to Southwest Asia, where they provided refueling support for coalition aircraft as part of Operation Desert Storm. While in Saudi Arabia, the wing air-delivered food to the Kurds in Northern Iraq from April to May 1991. Typical of the aircrews deployed were, from left to right, Stan Norris, Steve Base, Troy Warner, and Mark Kennedy.

Judy Babcock and Rex Schlagenhauf of the 305th AREFS are planning a refueling mission in 1991. Mary Higgins, not pictured, became the first female aircrew member at Grissom in 1977. Eighteen other women had been selected for pilot training in what was considered a test program. The idea was successful, and in 1993, combat aircraft positions were open to women. By 2014, the Air Force had 678 female pilots and 272 female navigators.

Many of the Soviet republics declared their independence in the early 1990s, and East and West Germany were reunited. Virtually broke, the Russians were powerless to preserve their empire, and in September 1991, Pres. George H.W. Bush ordered SAC to stand down its ground alert. Two months later, the Soviet Union ceased to exist when the Russian Republic formed the Commonwealth of Independent States. The Cold War was over.

Four

THE KLAXON CALL

Cocked and ready for war, a third of Bunker Hill and Grissom's fleet of bombers and tankers was on constant alert.

Soviet bombers and submarines, presumably armed with nuclear weapons, probed the US early-warning system. America's only defense was a strong offense that could survive an attack and then retaliate in what was understood to be a war of "mutually assured destruction." But to survive the first blow and remain a credible deterrent, SAC's aircraft had to get airborne fast.

The Strategic Air Command was a highly trained and disciplined organization. Aviation historian Alwyn T. Lloyd wrote that after Gen. Curtis LeMay took over as SAC commander in October 1948, rigorous training programs and competitions were instituted to keep the crewmen sharp. "He created the Spot Promotion program in which an entire crew was promoted one grade for winning the Bomb Comp," says Lloyd. "If any member of a crew committed a major operational infraction, the entire crew was busted back one grade." An airman who had been indoctrinated in Lemay's training and discipline was said to be "SACumcised."

At Bunker Hill, Hustler pilot Jack Strank explained that alert crews always stayed together:

> Whenever a crew left the (alert) facility to go to the BX, Commissary, simulator, one of the clubs, church, they had to sign out so that the CQ knew their location. The crews were allowed some freedom but were restricted to only the area that were so many minutes from the alert barracks; this was to conform to the desired response time to answer an alert. We could even play golf but had to have someone follow us around the course in an alert vehicle so that we could respond to an alert in the required time. Headquarters SAC knew the strain and stress put on the crews and really tried to make alert duty as comfortable and pleasant as possible. After our week on alert we would have Saturday and Sunday off and usually fly on Monday or Tuesday.

If SAC personnel weren't on alert, they were likely either flying or training in a team-oriented environment.

Everything on a SAC base revolved around the alert klaxon. When the flashing lights and sirens went off, everybody who was essential to the wing's mission had a place to be and less than 15 minutes to be there.

The Alert Facility was a concrete and steel, mostly underground hotel where flight crews and support personnel lived with their airplanes. A security policeman monitored the alarmed perimeter fence from a tower, and heavily armed sentries stood guard on each airplane. Officially classified as a "no-lone zone," nobody was allowed around an aircraft alone, and nobody got close to an airplane without proper authorization. The use of deadly force was authorized in the event that security protocols were broken.

SAC first placed aircraft and crews on alert status in 1957 to present a deterrence against the possibility of a Communist attack. To insure their readiness, the crew runs through their complete preflight checklists every day. In 1977, KC-135 pilot Larry Thomas, left, and copilot William Estelle are double-checking that their airplane is ready if called upon to go to war.

Each B-58 had a four-man support crew while on alert status. Working in pairs, because it took two men to move the ladder stand, these teams stayed with their aircraft for 24 hours, then had 24 hours off and repeated the schedule as long as their bomber remained cocked. The aircraft in this picture was not on alert because only the pilot was permitted to enter the cockpit of a cocked bomber. (Courtesy of Arley Brewer.)

SAC acknowledged that a single multimegaton bomb detonated above a SAC base would almost certainly destroy the bombers based there. The retaliatory force could only expect to survive an

attack if it were in the air before the missiles arrived. Fifteen minutes was all they had. In 1961, SAC ordered every wing to be airborne capable in 15 minutes or less. (Courtesy of US Air Force.)

Cocked and ready for war, this KC-135A has been outfitted with thermal curtains to protect the crew from the flash of an atomic blast, rollover chocks to allow for immediate taxi, and a breech cap, which was used on the A model tankers, to hold an explosive charge that started the engines quickly. (Courtesy of Paul Coffey.)

SAC tested the capability of the units to execute the emergency war plan through a no-notice Operational Readiness Inspection (ORI). Typically, the SAC inspector general would arrive at the base and present the wing commander with an execution order for a simulated emergency war plan mission. Alert crews were evaluated first in their ability to get to their airplanes and start the engines.

The entire wing was then required to generate the remainder of the bombers and tankers to full wartime, combat-ready status. Throughout the 1960s, the exercise included loading the Hustlers with their nuclear weapons. Inspectors carefully briefed personnel at the conclusion of the inspection, which often lasted a week. Failure to meet the necessarily demanding SAC standards would result in an end to the wing commander's career.

The sound of the alert klaxon and the roar of jet engines never failed to get everybody's attention. This was what they had trained for but never hoped to do. Within hours, word would have spread throughout the base that the nation was still at peace and that the ORI team was here. Still, everyone stayed tense after the drill. (Courtesy of the *Peru Tribune*.)

The increased level of activity continued day and night all over the base as every organization, from the kitchen staff to the police force, was tested in war-condition standards. Inspectors attempted to penetrate secure areas, created simulated crashes on the runway, and counted rations to determine how long the wing could remain self-sufficient.

The ORI, combined with annual evaluations by the Air Force inspector general, contributed significantly to SAC's readiness and proficiency and represented the highest standards of any command in the US Air Force. SAC personnel willingly accepted this challenge because they understood there was simply too much at stake to do otherwise.

Alert aircraft receive a complete preflight inspection by the crew chief and the aircraft commander every morning. Short of actually starting the engines, every system and component on the airplane is physically inspected. Any irregularities result in a fresh airplane joining the alert force while the broken one is dearmed and repaired. Dave Peed (kneeling) and Sid Kubesch are preflighting the *Greased Lightning*. (Courtesy of Col. Sid Kubesch.)

Flight crews ordinarily remained an intact family as long as everybody stayed in the same wing. People came and went from alert status every seven days, but the aircraft would often remain cocked through extended periods. Part of the ritual of changing KC-135 alert crews involved the weekly "bag exchange," where in order to keep the airplane ready, flight crews would load the aircraft with personal items they might need for war.

Alert aircraft were fully armed and cocked. By the mid-1960s, the B-58s sported a new two-component pod (TCP) system that used twin stacked pods, with the upper pod carrying a variable yield nuclear weapon and the lower pod amounting to a big drop tank that would be discarded during an operational mission once exhausted of fuel. In this rare photograph, the weapons pod has already been attached. (Courtesy of Arley Brewer.)

Navigator John Witzel tunes radar equipment as part of his checklist duties aboard a KC-135 in 1977. In order to expand the KC-135's capabilities and improve its reliability, the aircraft has undergone a number of modifications and technological upgrades. Among these was the Pacer-CRAG program (compass, radar, and GPS), which ran from 1999 until 2002 and replaced the crew navigator with new technology.

Just one of the five bombs carried aboard a B-58 burns at 7,000 degrees during detonation and reduces everything within 20 miles to molten, radioactive sand. Such terrible potential places a tremendous responsibility on anybody who even comes near these airplanes. These technicians are loading a mission pod aboard a Hustler. (Courtesy of Arley Brewer.)

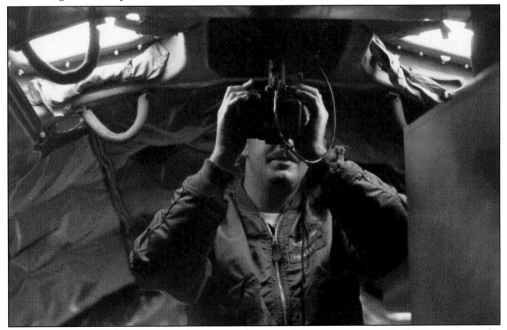

Former B-58 pilot Jack Strank said that, among his crew, "the navigator was the busiest man on the airplane." The same description held true for the tanker crews. In the days before GPS satellites, the boom operator used a periscope sextant to help the navigator verify the aircraft's location. Calibrations like this were part of the preflight checks performed aboard the alert aircraft.

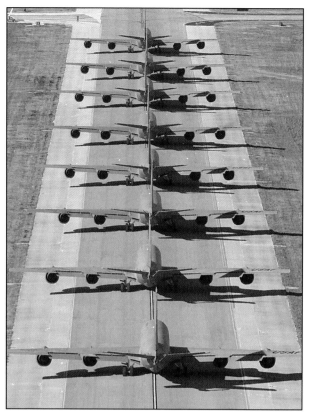

Minimum Interval Takeoff is a technique used by SAC to get bombers and tankers airborne and away from the base, scrambling all available aircraft at 12- and 15-second intervals. Before takeoff, the aircraft taxi to the runway in what has come to be known as an elephant walk. This procedure is designed to maximize the number of aircraft launched before the base faced a nuclear strike.

Pres. George H.W. Bush announced that "recent developments in the Soviet Union represented historic opportunities to change fundamental and nuclear posture of both the United States and the Soviet Union that will increase stability and reduce the risk of war." The next day, Saturday, September 28, 1991, Grissom went off alert. Pictured are the empty alert pads, the munitions storage area, and security police training area.

Five

VICTORY

Grissom Air Force Base entered the 1990s with a feeling of uncertainty about its future. As the Soviet Union continued to collapse, the Pentagon announced more and more cutbacks in military spending. The alert crews stood down and went home to their families in September 1991 while ground crews stayed behind on the ramp, downloading their aircraft. SAC headquarters specifically ordered that the Alert Facility be locked, which was an interesting idea since there were no locks on any of the doors. While tankers were being towed to the other side of the runway, the civil engineers fashioned padlocks to secure the facility.

The inevitable approach of another Indiana winter drew a dark and somber curtain across Grissom. Airmen began to disappear through transfers or separation from the Air Force. No one came in their place. Dormitory rooms emptied, and moving vans wandered around the maze of housing area streets in search of addresses. Cold aircraft sat on the ramp. It was just too much for a little dog, who had already lost one family, to watch helplessly while the place she had adopted as home began to crumble around her.

With the Cold War officially won, a large deterrent force was no longer needed. On June 1, 1992, the Air Force shoved its mailed fist holding bolts of lightening with an olive branch into a pocket and turned all refueling units over to the new Air Mobility Command (AMC), merging former SAC air refueling aircraft with strategic and tactical theater airlift aircraft. The wing that earned fame as Curtis LeMay's 305th Bomb Group slipped quietly and peacefully into the 305th Air Mobility Wing (305th AMW) on October 1, 1994.

The era of the Strategic Air Command was over.

Grissom Air Force Base was turned over to the Air Force Reserve, as the 305th Air Refueling Wing phased-out operations in 1994. The KC-135R-equipped 70th and 305th Air Refueling Squadrons were inactivated. In addition, the EC-135G/L radio-relay aircraft, as part of the Post Attack Command and Control System, were also retired.

Somewhere out along the runway in October 1994, a lonesome little dog watched the wing move its flag to McGuire Air Force Base, New Jersey, leaving her, the remaining personnel, and aircraft behind.

Known in 1992 simply as the 45th Fighter Squadron (FS), because the Department of the Air Force decided that "Tactical Fighter Squadron" seemed a bit redundant, Grissom's Warthogs came to be known as the "Hoosier Hogs," part of the 930th Fighter Group.

The 45th Fighter Squadron's operations desk is seen near the end of its usefulness. From left to right are Chris Fesler, Andy Duffin, Jack Ross, Mike Gleichman, and John Dodge in April 1994. This area, like some of the airmen in this picture, would soon become something else. Squadron operations is the center of flight activity, including scheduling, planning, and mission briefing. Indiana congressman Steve Buyer had announced in February 1994 that Grissom would be realigned and the 45th FS deactivated. (Courtesy of Tim Cahoon.)

Frank Countryman leans on the deadly 30mm rotary cannon in the nose of a 45th TFS A-10. This particular airplane was paired with its namesake, a World War II P-47 Thunderbolt in a series of aerial photo shoots, commemorating the 50th anniversary of the D-Day invasion. The Air Force gave unusual permission for the 45th to repaint this A-10 in P-47 regalia with the bold white stripes used to distinguish friendly from enemy aircraft during the 1944 invasion of Normandy. (Courtesy of Tim Cahoon.)

A Saber Arch is a military tradition in which sabers or swords are used to salute a newly married couple. The bride and groom pass under an honorary arch of sabers, typically when exiting the building in which the wedding ceremony took place. June 28, 1994, marked the final flight of a Grissom based A-10 Thunderbolt II. The base fire department is saluting the event, and the 45th TFS, with a less-traditional water cannon arch. (Courtesy of Tim Cahoon.)

Representing Grissom's aviation lineage, a vintage Navy trainer taxis past a huge KC-135R during an invitational fly-in sponsored by the Grissom Air Museum. The Boeing Stearman PT-17s date to 1934 and flew from Bunker Hill during World War II. The jet-powered, 161-ton KC-135 came along in 1956 and supported combat operations during the Vietnam and Desert Storm wars.

A-10 pilot Ozzie Gorbitz helps Tim Cahoon unstrap after landing from his last flight at Grissom in May 1994. Late spring was the last time most of these airmen would work and fly together, as Grissom and most of the 45th Fighter Squadron were shut down. The crew chief on this airplane was Terry Rogers, who is not pictured. (Courtesy of Tim Cahoon.)

As the 45th Tactical Fighter Squadron shuttered its doors at Grissom, a handful of leftovers deployed to Aviano Air Base, Italy, to participate in NATO's Operation Deny Flight, a NATO-ordered no-fly zone over Bosnia and Herzegovina. The mission was later expanded to include providing close air support for United Nations troops and carrying out coercive air strikes against targets in Bosnia. Twelve NATO members contributed forces to the operation, and by its end on December 20, 1995, NATO pilots had flown 100,420 sorties. (Courtesy of Tim Cahoon.)

What had been the largest and undeniably best-trained command in the US Air Force was deactivated in 1992. 434th Operations Group commander Brian Dobbert is recognized by the base fire department after his last flight. In 1994, the 305th Aerial Refueling Wing left Grissom for McGuire AFB, New Jersey.

When all is said and done...
Gus proves legends come in all sizes

By SSgt. Katherine Gandara
305th Public Affairs Office

Grissom lost an important member of the family recently. One who had been part of the base for more than a decade.

A little vagabond dog, known to many as Gus (dubbed in honor of base namesake, astronaut Lt. Col. Virgil "Gus" Grissom), died. Every Air Force base has a unique spirit and Gus gave Grissom a distinctive character for more than 12 years.

Security police found the black and tan body of the well-known mascot on a wintery weekend morning in front of Grissom's personnel building.

"I got a call to respond to a dead animal, never imagining it was Gus," said SrA. William Engelter, 305th Security Police Squadron. "When I found Gus, there was such an overwhelming feeling of disappointment. Even though Gus didn't officially belong to anyone, that little dog was everyone's pet."

Gus' death, much like the tiny dog's life, remains a mystery. There was even a raging debate on gender. Majority opinion was that Gus was actually a Gussie, but the plain truth was Gus was Gus no matter what.

No one really knew where the plucky pooch came from, yet plenty of stories about Gus' origins abound. Some say a base family left Gus behind years ago. Others believe Gus was just a stray that wandered onto base and claimed Grissom as

Photo by TSgt. Rick Gracia

Gus called Grissom home for more than 12 years.

home.

Through the years, the furry tramp's timeworn paws beat a busy and familiar path around favorite stomping grounds. Base residents spotted Gus roaming the housing area

---

"Even though Gus didn't officially belong to anyone, that little dog was everyone's pet."

**SrA. William Engelter,
305th Security Police Squadron**

---

one minute and in the blink of an eye the nimble-footed canine would be jaunting along the flightline periphery.

Gus was a regular visitor to the maintenance areas and dining facility where big-hearted folks made sure the celebrity mongrel never went hungry.

"I was running the flightline perimeter road

when I noticed Gus running alongside with a huge chunk of bologna in its mouth," said 1st Lt. Ed Bachl, 305th Air Refueling Wing executive officer. "Gus trotted along side until a security police truck came

into the horizon. In an instant, Gus was gone."

The pint-sized fugitive continually outmaneuvered the base law. It was almost like Gus had a sixth sense and knew when security police were in the area. Catching the tiny outlaw represented a formidable challenge to Grissom peacekeepers who never quit trying -- or maybe Gus'

legend influenced their efforts more than the dog's elusive nature.

"My wife, Jo, spotted Gus the first day we got to Grissom," said Col. Marc Drinkhahn, 305th ARW commander. "An avid animal lover, she called the security police to report what she thought was someone's lost pet. The desk sergeant knew it was Gus before she had given a complete description. The sergeant told her the mythical mutt had been eluding capture for years."

How did such a diminutive soul etch a lasting impression on so many people?

Perhaps Gus embodied the very essence of the characteristics that distinguish the men and women of the Air Force. Gus was perseverant, resilient, adaptable, and a real scrapper. Gus was a sort of kindred spirit everyone could identify with.

Air Force members have made and been a part of history, and felt firsthand the effects of the changing military climate. Along the way, Gus symbolized the unwavering strength of his/her adopted military family.

Gus' death was an unexpected awakening of sorts. Many thought a little of the 305th would live on with Gus. Even though Gus left early, he taught the lesson that legends come in all sizes. It's not how big the memory is but the quality of it that keeps Gus' memory alive.(**Courtesy 305th ARW Public Affairs**)

The spirit of Grissom Air Force Base curled up on the sidewalk outside base personnel like she was waiting for somebody, and bid her adopted Air Force family farewell. A memorial to Gus is located in front of the Grissom Air Museum, reminding every veteran of what was left behind.

Six

LEGACIES

The SAC Operational Readiness Inspection team arrived at Bunker Hill AFB in the early stages of a snowstorm on Tuesday, December 8, 1964. Alert crews had been cooped up together since Friday when the klaxon sent them sprinting for their aircraft. While his wife, Virginia, was at home planning Christmas for the family, Capt. Manuel "Rocky" Cervantes climbed the stairs to his bomber and strapped himself into history.

As he aligned his sophisticated navigational systems, Rocky began decoding the emergency action message, which might direct the crew to launch. Hot exhaust blasted from behind each engine as Capt. Leary Johnson, the pilot of B-58 serial number 60-1116, quickly went through his starting checklist on the airplane's intercom with Capt. Roger Hall, the defense systems operator. The crew lowered their overhead hatches just as the crew chiefs pushed the boarding stairs clear, and Johnson taxied out to the runway. Their bomber would be at the end of a line of aircraft launching eight seconds apart.

Alert crews were regularly scrambled under simulated wartime conditions to make sure that they could launch in the required 15 minutes. Jack Strank, Leary Johnson, and everybody else waiting in line to launch that morning were focused on only one thing, getting airborne.

Johnson would later testify that he "saw a flash and the airplane lurched to the left." Then, Hall looked out his small window over the wing and saw flames. Johnson ordered his crew to abandon their aircraft. Three hatch covers blew away as the crew initiated emergency egress procedures. Johnson and Hall escaped with minor burns when they were able to climb out of the burning bomber, jump to the ground, and roll in the snow. But Rocky was trapped in the middle of the airplane and completely surrounded by flames.

"Let us remember that Capt. Cervantes died in helping preserve our freedom by demonstrating his ability as a freedom warrior. He is just as much a casualty as if he were killed in a shooting war," read a December 11, 1964, editorial by the *Indianapolis Star*.

Manuel "Rocky" Cervantes, of Dallas, Texas, joined the Air Force in 1955 and received his commission in May 1956 through the Aviation Cadet Program. Seen at far right in this picture, he trained as an aircrew navigator at Ellington Air Force Base near Houston. (Courtesy of Shamaine Pleczko.)

Cervantes was selected for B-47 bombers and assigned to the 509th Bomb Wing at Whiteman Air Force Base, Missouri. He had accumulated more than 1,000 hours in the B-47 before being chosen for Hustler duty and transferred to Bunker Hill in January 1962. Rocky is on the far right and is pictured with his B-47 crew. (Courtesy of Shamaine Pleczko.)

"I'll never die that way," Rocky vowed to a friend after Hustler crewmen William Berry and William Bergdoll burned to death in a fiery accident at Bunker Hill in August 1963. During the 10-year operational life of the Hustler, 17 Bunker Hill and Grissom airmen died in accidents involving 11 bombers.

Rocky raised his overhead hatch to find himself completely surrounded by 14,000 gallons of burning jet fuel. His only hope of escape was the rocket propelled ejection pod. The pod would close to form a relatively safe cocoon and then blast him out of his burning airplane. Extremely effective at high speeds and high altitude, the capsule was not safe for a runway ejection because the parachute would not have time to open at ground level.

According to the accident report, submitted by Gen. Everett Holstrom, former commander of the 43rd Bomb Wing, "the high explosives in all five weapons detonated. The aircraft and weapons wreckage burned for two hours." During recovery operations the next day, the secondary on one of the nuclear weapons burst into flames and was buried in sand. "The next day," now two days after the wreck, "when this secondary was moved it ignited again," said General Holstrom. (Courtesy of Craig Trott.)

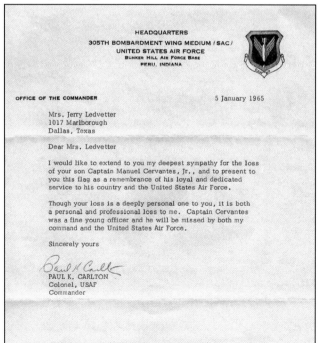

305th Wing commander Paul Carlton reported the accident to SAC headquarters as a "Broken Arrow." Throughout the Cold War, the Air Force reported 32 Broken Arrows, including this accident at Bunker Hill; a Broken Arrow meant a burning nuclear weapon and radioactive contamination. James Andrews and Alexander Hydak were treated for smoke inhalation, and firefighter Isaac Brown was hospitalized with a shoulder injury during rescue operations. (Courtesy of Shamaine Pleczko.)

The exact cause of the bizarre accident remains a mystery. SAC never assessed blame for Rocky's death, and a popular theory is that jet blast from the aircraft in front of 60-1116 blew Rocky's airplane backwards on the icy runway where a runway light ruptured a fuel tank. (Courtesy of Craig Trott.)

The Air Force allowed news media on the base after the fire was extinguished and reported "no danger of radiation." While reporters interviewed Johnson and Hall at the base hospital, munitions specialists carted the leaking thermonuclear weapons to an open field south of the runway, where they were buried. A few days later, engineers buried the rest of the wreckage. The weapons were transferred to disposal facilities in Tennessee and Texas on December 22, 1964. (Courtesy of Craig Trott.)

A 1991 Air Force investigation, conducted at the request of Congress, revealed two radioactive sites on Grissom. The first was an area between the alert pads and runway and suspected to be the site of the 1964 accident. The other site was the location of the buried wreckage. In 2000, the Air Force remediated the sites and recovered from the area south of the runway a number of aircraft parts, including a B-58 ejection capsule seat. (Courtesy of the Indiana Department of Environmental Management.)

This photograph, revealing the empty alert pads after SAC was deactivated in 1992, also illustrates the taxiway connecting the alert pads to the runway. This is where Rocky's bomber was blown into a runway light by jet blast from another aircraft. It was here that the burning thermonuclear weapons were initially buried, and the site was later determined to be radioactive.

Rocky died at the base hospital about an hour after his airplane exploded. He was 29 years old, and it was two weeks before Christmas. Waiting for him at home was his wife, Virginia, his sons, Manuel (six years old) and Michael (five years old), and his daughter, Shamaine (six months old). (Courtesy of Shamaine Pleczko.)

After SAC had been deactivated, the aerial refueling responsibilities of the US Air Force were assumed by the new Air Mobility Command. Maj. Gen. Walter Kross, AMC commander, is welcomed to Grissom by security policemen David Perry and Kalvix Thornton. The 305th Air Refueling Wing was transferred without aircraft to McGuire Air Force Base, New Jersey, on October 1, 1994, and redesignated the 305th Air Mobility Wing.

A "secret" security clearance, a restricted area badge, and a reason to be there were all required to get inside the heavily guarded primary alert area. With weeds sprouting around the padlocked Alert Facility, the entry control point remains a ghostly sentry of the "Can Do" legacy. (Author's collection.)

When the Navy left Bunker Hill in 1946, a committee of local businessmen, consisting mostly of farmers, worked to find new uses for the facilities. Building S-16 in "Operations Circle" across the street from base operations became a family restaurant in September 1947. Delco Electronics, a division of General Motors, occupied the building in the background. (Courtesy of Craig Trott.)

Once a beehive of activity, and still adorned with the distinctive checkerboard, base operations is shown shuttered and cold on a crisp afternoon in May 2014. This photograph was taken in front of where S-16 once stood in Operations Circle. The row of buildings in the previous picture have long been demolished. (Author's collection.)

Only eight of the 116 B-58s survive today. This Hustler, one of the first to be modified as a trainer and consequently designated a TB-58, is on static display at the Grissom Air Museum. Located just outside what once served as the main gate, the museum hosts 23 military aircraft and other exhibits that preserve the proud legacy of Bunker Hill and Grissom Air Force Base. (Courtesy of Leroy Miller.)

Visitors to the Grissom Air Museum can see a variety of military aircraft landing at the still very active reserve base.

William Menges, in this Huey helicopter pilot's seat, goes through the start-up checklist with his grandsons Will Imbierowicz and Jacob Patty. The helicopter is one of several hands-on exhibits at the Grissom Air Museum. (Courtesy of Marty Menges.)

Addy Robb inspects a mock cockpit of an F-16 fighter jet at the Grissom Air Museum in 2015. A very popular hands-on exhibit, F-16s were never assigned at Grissom, and this simulator is decorated in the 305th Bomb Wing livery of a B-58 Hustler. Hustlers never wore but certainly helped earn this fuselage ribbon, a Cold War Victory medal. (Author's collection.)

Safe ramp tower once overlooked the primary alert area where security police monitored intrusion alarms on the ground and along the perimeter fence. Today, the tower guards the Grissom Museum's collection of aircraft spanning 80 years of military history. (Author's collection.)

Jon Kitchel grew up on his family's farm just two miles west of Grissom and was characteristically oblivious to the military air traffic while concentrating on his soybean crop in 2010. The base had always seemed dangerously mysterious with the barbed-wire fences, heavily armed security, and threatening perimeter signs. But outside the fence, a Hoosier farm family works through a warm harvest afternoon. (Courtesy of Terry Wyant.)

Air Force One brought President Obama and Vice President Biden to Kokomo, via Grissom Air Reserve Base, in November 2010.

Throughout the Cold War, while the Soviets challenged and tested the resolve of the United States in places like Korea, Cuba, and Vietnam, the United States never suffered a direct attack. Enemies understood that any assault on US homeland would unleash a devastating counterattack with horrible consequences. While the men and women assigned to SAC's Bunker Hill and Grissom Air Force Base were always prepared for war, peace was their profession.

Discover Thousands of Local History Books Featuring Millions of Vintage Images

Arcadia Publishing, the leading local history publisher in the United States, is committed to making history accessible and meaningful through publishing books that celebrate and preserve the heritage of America's people and places.

Find more books like this at
www.arcadiapublishing.com

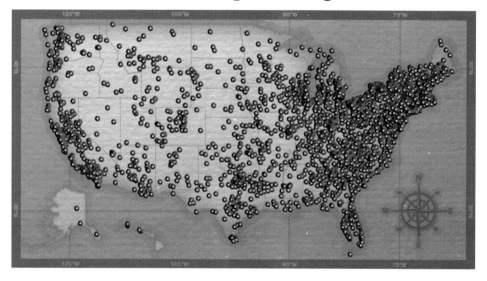

Search for your hometown history, your old stomping grounds, and even your favorite sports team.

Consistent with our mission to preserve history on a local level, this book was printed in South Carolina on American-made paper and manufactured entirely in the United States. Products carrying the accredited Forest Stewardship Council (FSC) label are printed on 100 percent FSC-certified paper.

MADE IN THE USA